The Hostess Handbook

A Modern Guide to Entertaining
with 100 Recipes for Every Occasion

Maria Zizka

PHOTOGRAPHS BY ERIN SCOTT

Artisan Books | New York

Library of Congress Cataloging-in-Publication Data
Names: Zizka, Maria, author. | Scott, Erin, photographer.
   Title: The hostess handbook : a modern guide to entertaining
   / Maria Zizka ; photographs by Erin Scott.
Description: New York : Artisan Books, [2024] | Includes bibliographical
   references and index.
Identifiers: LCCN 2023042591 | ISBN 9781648291807 (hardcover)
Subjects: LCSH: Cooking. | Entertaining. | LCGFT: Cookbooks.
Classification: LCC TX714 .Z594 2024 | DDC 642/.4—dc23/eng/20231116
LC record available at https://lccn.loc.gov/2023042591

Design by Graham Bradley and Nina Simoneaux
Lettering by Graham Bradley

Artisan books may be purchased in bulk for business, educational, or promotional use. For information, please contact your local bookseller or the Hachette Book Group Special Markets Department at special.markets@hbgusa.com.

The publisher is not responsible for websites (or their content) that are not owned by the publisher.

The Hachette Speakers Bureau provides a wide range of authors for speaking events. To find out more, go to hachettespeakersbureau.com or email HachetteSpeakers@hbgusa.com.

Published by Artisan,
an imprint of Workman Publishing,
a division of Hachette Book Group, Inc.
1290 Avenue of the Americas
New York, NY 10104
artisanbooks.com

The Artisan name and logo are registered trademarks of Hachette Book Group, Inc.

Printed in China on responsibly sourced paper

First printing, April 2024

10 9 8 7 6 5 4 3 2 1

Cheers to the cooks, the party
people, the birthday cake bakers,
and everyone who loves to celebrate
with delicious food and drinks

CONTENTS

Party Snacks

Starters

Sides & Salads

Mains

Desserts

Drinks

Menus

Introduction

You might think that hosting a party requires a closetful of matching plates and silverware, plus enough stemmed glassware to serve twenty. You might think your home has to be so beautiful that it could be featured in a magazine for its stylish interior design in order for guests to feel comfortable. And you might be led to believe that you need to somehow possess the skills of both a Cordon Bleu–trained restaurant chef and a professional event planner to orchestrate a delicious meal for a crowd. But I'm here to say that you don't actually need any of that.

In fact, overly coordinated parties usually end up feeling a little cold or impersonal. My guess is that you're not trying to organize a conference meeting in a drab ballroom. You want fun, spontaneity, boisterous laughter, food that's so delicious people swarm around it. You want the warmth and comfort of someone's home, the glowy feeling of a celebration that just keeps getting better and better, one that you hope never ends.

For those kinds of parties, you need only three things: the desire to host, some reliably excellent go-to recipes, and a bit of party know-how. It really is that simple, I promise. Everything else is just bonus. With those three pillars in place, you will be ready to host parties that your friends and family will love and talk about for years.

This book will show you how to plan your own fantastic menu, how to get your space party-ready, and how to welcome anywhere from two to twenty guests all while enjoying the festivities yourself. Because isn't enjoying the party one of the hardest parts of hosting? The best party foods are things you can eat with your hands while holding a drink and chatting with friends and family. Recipes for Party

Snacks (pages 20 to 39) and Starters (pages 42 to 81) will give you plenty of options to nibble on as the party gets started. For larger gatherings, when everyone is seated around a big table, Sides and Salads (pages 84 to 133) help fill out a well-balanced menu, plus it feels so convivial to pass platters of beautiful food. And who can resist reaching for a deliciously appetizing starter such as a steaming-hot Saffron Arancini (page 79) as it passes by in front of you? There's a lot to think about and coordinate for a party, so the Mains (pages 138 to 191) should be easy to make ahead and ideally flexible enough that you could double the recipe with success or try a variation. Once you try the Potato Chip–Crust Chicken with Green Olive Relish (page 162), your friends might request it for every future dinner party.

Nothing says celebration quite like Desserts (pages 194 to 241). I don't believe in restricting candles only to birthdays, and definitely not only to cakes. Anniversaries, work promotions, accomplished goals, even the start of a new school year—these all deserve candlelit celebrations, whether you are sticking candles in Giant Pavlova with Chamomile Cream and Citrus (page 213) or Dulce de Leche Gelato Affogato (page 236).

Last but not least, Drinks (pages 244 to 267) are necessary for a good party. You can't go wrong with tried-and-true favorites, from a Classic Martini (page 254) to Frozen Margarita (page 259), but follow the tips in the recipes to turn these drinks into batch cocktails, pick up a few bartending secrets, and try the variations for festive garnishes. There are many reasons why someone might not be drinking alcohol, and you'll find plenty of recipes for nonalcoholic drinks. Making a wonderful nonalcoholic drink is a little trickier than simply leaving out the booze. These recipes will show you how to mix drinks that everyone will want.

If you've ever felt confused about navigating guests' various dietary restrictions, you are not alone! It can sometimes seem like solving a puzzle if one guest is a vegetarian, another avoids dairy, and a few can't have gluten. But fear not, limitations often lead to the most creative results. When you figure out the perfect menu to suit eaters of all kinds, and when every guest is cared for and generously fed, you'll revel in the feelings of mutual love around the party table. That warmth is worth the extra attention given to the menu. The recipes in this book are considerate of dietary restrictions and always offer suggestions for how to adjust ingredients as needed.

Of course, hosting isn't just about cooking a great meal. Tucked in among the recipes are all the advice and party tricks you'll need to make your guests feel welcomed and keep yourself calm, cool, and collected. Ever wondered how to make fresh-cut flowers look their best for days? Check out All About Flowers (page 242). Do you find yourself questioning on which side of the plate to place the fork and knife or how much food is enough food? Read through Setting the Table (page 82) and The Art of Serving (page 135). Plus, beginning on page 270, you'll find a special selection of curated menus for a variety of inspired parties. There's a Friends and Family Sunday Supper (page 278), a lovely Galentine's (or Valentine's) Day meal (page 274) to share with friends or lovers, a new take on the Game Day buffet (page 282), an epic holiday feast (page 290), and a Springtime Luncheon (page 277),

perfect for celebrating mothers, brides to be, babies on the way, or simply the coming of spring. On page 192, you can also find a simple three-step plan for putting together your own custom menu.

Like the lead-up to a vacation, the preparation for a party is often a time full of excitement, anticipation, and limitless potential. The spark of the idea to host. The moment when you've figured out what you'd like to cook. Even the tidying up of your home, making it shine with invitation. There's so much pleasure and joy to be found as you go about tending to all the details. You do all these tasks with an open heart. You try to create something beautiful, something meaningful, for others. When you're getting everything party-ready, you might even consider bringing a friend along to the farmers' market or to shop for wine (and why not taste some wine while you're there?). Make the process fun and you're really creating two parties in one.

I hope this cookbook inspires you to host parties in style and with ease. Always remember that when the host is having a good time, the guests will, too.

Party Supplies

Do you need fine china and a fully stocked chef's kitchen to be an excellent host? Absolutely not! In fact, it's likely you have all the supplies needed to start cooking for friends and family, so feel free to skip right ahead to the recipes! You really can make do with whatever you have. However, investing in a few kitchen tools, some beloved serving trays, and a few extra plates and glasses can take a lot of stress out of hosting. Here's a list of items you might want to have on hand when planning your next party. Check out the alternatives suggested for when you're in a pinch, borrow anything you can from friends and neighbors, and keep your eye out for antique stores and garage sales. You'll be amazed by the pristine Dutch ovens still in their boxes that you can find.

COOKWARE

Sheet Pans

The humble rimmed metal sheet pan just might be the kitchen hero when cooking for a crowd. You can roast vegetables on it. You can bake cookies on it. You can use it to store ingredients you've prepped. The pans with rimmed edges are best because they'll contain any juicy dribbles. See if you can find a sturdy sheet pan (shop online or in a restaurant supply store), and it'll last for years without warping. The most common one you'll come across is 18 by 13 inches (46 by 33 cm), which is called a half-sheet pan in restaurant-speak (the full sheet pan fits commercial ovens but is too big for home kitchens). Try to also get your hands on a couple of quarter-sheet pans (13 by 9 inches/33 by 23 cm). They are endlessly useful for smaller-scale tasks.

Dutch Oven

The heavy, enameled cast-iron pot with handles on the sides that's known as a Dutch oven is wonderful for cooking big saucy pastas, braises, and so much more. These pots are so gorgeous—especially when they've been used and loved and taken on a patina—that they can go from stovetop to oven to dining table.

IN A PINCH:

- A large pot with a lid (ideally all metal parts so it can go in the oven)

TABLEWARE

Boards and Platters

The board or platter is the ultimate vehicle for sharing or presenting a dish to guests. A couple of large-scale platters to serve dishes like elegantly composed salads and hearty main courses to a crowd are worth the investment. Boards and platters are also useful for offering appetizers

and bite-size starters like Brown Butter Roasted Radish Toasts (page 60). Some cutting boards are pretty enough to chop on in the kitchen and then bring directly to the table. Remember that wooden boards will be stained by certain foods: turmeric, beets, even sliced strawberries can leave behind tinted shadows. If you're worried about stains, you can always lay down a sheet of parchment paper under a dish like Turmeric- and Beet-Pickled Deviled Eggs (page 49). And it's probably best not to cut on any special boards that you don't want to show knife blade marks. Save the prep for your workhorse cutting boards.

IN A PINCH:

- A sheet pan lined with parchment paper
- A ceramic baking dish or pie dish

Enamel Bowls, Plates, and Cups

Especially great when you're celebrating outdoors, enamel plates and cups are lightweight and sturdy. They're nearly unbreakable—even in the hands of toddlers—and yet, unlike a disposable plate, there is something undeniably special about using a real plate. Check garage sales and antique stores for vintage enamelware, which often comes in beautiful and less commonly available colors. Plus, a little patina on enamelware only adds to the charm.

Disposables and Eco-Partyware

For picnics and other outdoor parties, nobody wants to tote along heavy ceramic plates, fine silverware, and breakable glasses. But how do you capture the convenience of tossing all the dirty plates and used cups into the nearest trash bin without feeling the guilt of waste? Thankfully, these days, there are tons of great options for compostable plates, forks, spoons, knives, cups, and napkins made from bamboo, wood fiber,

can consider eco-friendly disposables, of course, but also many party foods don't require forks or knives, and you can plan your menu around the number and type of utensils you have. In other words, work with what you've got. A large spoon and fork make a fine substitute for salad tongs, which can often actually be rather unwieldy. For serving spoons, look for affordable vintage serveware with character at thrift shops and antique stores.

IN A PINCH:

- Toothpicks—aka party picks—can stand in, literally, to spear through a Broiled Bratwurst Bite (page 71) or a pickle on a Charcuterie and Pickles Platter (page 36). And they also happen to be the perfect utensil for eating Toothpick Gnocchi with Oregano Bread Crumbs (page 113).
- Hands: Most starters and lots of side dishes are best enjoyed with your hands and maybe a napkin or two.

Glassware

As with utensils and plates, you don't need a huge amount of glassware to host fantastic parties. Don't stress about using specific glasses for the drink you're serving, such as a martini glass or a champagne flute (for more about glassware, see The Home Bar, page 268). Realistically, you simply need a water glass and a wine glass for every guest. And if you need to (or like to) mix and match your glasses, as a bonus, guests will have an easier time keeping track of which glass is theirs if it's unique. Look around at garage sales and in antique stores for beautiful, affordable glassware. When thinking about which kinds of glasses might be right for you, make sure to keep in mind the honest details of your life and home. Stackable glasses are useful in small spaces. Maybe you received a gorgeous set of fragile wine glasses as a wedding gift, but you also know they wouldn't stand a chance with a toddler at the table. Save them for later and seek

or sugarcane. They do usually cost a little bit more than their landfill-destined counterparts, but hot tip: You can often find them on sale during the off-season colder months. And even better, there are now lots of design and color choices, from scallop-edged plates to faux wood grain or speckled patterns, pretty pastels, and hues as bright as Starburst candy. To add another fun touch to your picnic table, try looking for plates in a fun shape—like ovals, hexagons, rectangles specifically sized for sushi rolls, and even short canoe-shaped bowls.

Utensils

You don't really need an unrealistically large set of utensils to host a big party. (For one thing, logistically, where do you even store a set of twenty-four forks?) You

out squat, nearly unbreakable glasses like
Duralex tumblers.

IN A PINCH:

- Recycled jars make lovely glasses (next
  time you're buying mustard or pickles, for
  example, keep your eye out for a jar you think
  would work well as a glass once you peel off
  the label and give it a good wash).

SERVING TRAYS

Serving trays are extremely useful for
parties. They can feel like a bit of a
throwback, but don't let that stop you
from using them. They're ideal for carrying
a stack of small plates and a few drinks
from the kitchen to another room. Also,
trays come in handy when you're cleaning
up after a party has ended. No need to
make a million trips between the table
and sink when you can simply stack and
carry on a tray! Whether you prefer sturdy
metallic handles or a sleek minimalist
design, there's a tray for everyone. If you're
shaking your head in disagreement, you
just haven't found your perfect tray yet.

IN A PINCH:

- A large cutting board
- For outdoor parties: the rigid top of a cooler

LINENS

What a joy it is to unfold a linen napkin and
lay it across your lap. That motion is like
a cue to your body that a delicious meal
is about to begin. Cloth napkins come in
every color and pattern under the sun. If
you're going for a party vibe that's casual
yet thoughtful, try setting the table with
various complementary but not matchy-
matchy cloth napkins. (For more about
tablecloths, see Setting the Table, page 82.)

IN A PINCH:

- Clean kitchen towels
- Fabric scraps (with their edges sewn if
  you like)

CAKE STANDS AND TOPPERS

A cake stand is meant for cake, obviously,
but that doesn't mean you can't serve a
grouping of cupcakes or a few clustered
stacks of cookies on one. Sturdy ones with
solid bases can even be used as elevated
cheese boards when placed on a table and
surrounded by other dishes. Varying the
height of dishes on a party table is always
a good idea for visual interest. Candles are
only the beginning when you start to think
about cake toppers. You can affix pom-
poms, paper flowers, and Polaroid photos
to thin bamboo skewers and stick them
in any kind of dessert. Think about what
or whom you're celebrating and then try
to come up with a unique and fun way to
honor the occasion.

IN A PINCH:

- A large, flat plate set atop an upside-down
  bowl (some combos balance better than
  others, obviously)

DECORATIONS

Balloons have long been a party decor
staple, but nobody wants their decorations
to come at a cost for the planet and,
unfortunately, latex balloons can take
four years or more to biodegrade. Instead,
choose an eco-friendly alternative like
tissue paper pom-poms, streamers, and
garlands (store-bought or homemade).
Bubbles are always a big hit with kids. And
you cannot go wrong with fresh flowers at
a party.

Hosting Checklist

☐ **Decide on the menu.** Give yourself at least one week in advance for a large, formal gathering. For impromptu parties, last-minute day-of decisions are totally fine.

☐ **Tidy your space.** Priority number one should be the bathroom. I suggest you clean in this order: (a) Make sure there's enough toilet paper and soap and put out a fresh hand towel. (b) Clear off the countertop by putting away any toiletries. (c) Spray and wipe down as many surfaces as you have time to reach. (d) If you can get to it, light a scented candle. Other areas in your home don't really need to be spotless. Your guests won't judge you if there are a few dishes in the sink. (In fact, I've watched my guests' shoulders visibly drop as they relax after seeing some dishes in the kitchen sink. Now I always make sure to leave a few plates unwashed—one of my best party tricks!)

☐ **Set the table.** A stack of plates, napkins, and forks on one side of the table is perfectly fine for casual parties. Just double-check that the things you need are clean and not languishing in the dishwasher, waiting for you to push the start button.

☐ **Ice!** Do you have it? If not, this can be a great task to assign to a friend who's coming to the party. They can pick up a bag on their way.

☐ **Is the playlist ready to go?** Start it up at a moderate volume before anyone arrives, and crank it louder later to keep the party energy flowing.

☐ **Bring any cheeses, olives, and charcuterie to room temperature.** They taste one hundred times better after they've shaken off the chill of the refrigerator.

☐ **Take a moment for yourself.** Maybe 15 minutes before the start time, change into your party outfit and do whatever you need to feel like the composed and stylish host that you are. Maybe you want to pour yourself a drink, even. There's nothing wrong with opening the first bottle of wine or mixing the first cocktail—you deserve it!

HOSTESS BINGO

Practice really does make perfect. And luckily, when it comes to hosting parties, the practicing part is fun. Mark off your accomplishments here as you work your way toward becoming the host with the most.

Mix a round of drinks like a pro *(see The Home Bar, page 268)*	Take the party outside—to the park, beach, garden, or rooftop	That fish you cooked left a lingering smell *(it's okay, see page 148)*	In a pinch, repurpose clean jars as glassware	Bring hungry friends home from the bar— spaghettata time! *(see page 241)*
Unexpected people arrive *(see 5 Ways with a Good Loaf of Bread, page 90, to stretch the meal)*	Somebody asks you to share a recipe	Prepare an impromptu appetizer *(see 10 Simple Nearly No-Cook Appetizers, page 63)*	Your table looks NICE! *(see Setting the Table, page 82)*	There's a round of applause as you carry the main course to the table
Party foul—red wine spill! *(don't worry, see page 266)*	Stick a candle in a non-cake dessert		Create your own custom menu *(see page 192 for ideas)*	Guests ask where you got this delicious wine *(see The Wine Guide, page 267)*
Drink in hand, you tidy up your space before guests arrive *(see the tips on page 18)*	Friends text to thank you for such a fun party	You introduce two new people and they hit it off	Guests linger because nobody wants the party to end	Wow! You styled that cheese board beautifully *(see page 35)*
GORGEOUS flowers on your table *(see All About Flowers, page 242)*	A glass breaks and you tell everyone that it's a sign of good luck	Well done! You outsourced dessert *(see page 232)*	Start dreaming about the next party before this one is over	Set the mood with the perfect playlist *(see page 67)*

Party Snacks

Party snacks are the little dishes you use to fill out a meal or add a nibble here and there. When guests arrive, offer something savory like Choose-Your-Own-Adventure Spiced Nuts (page 26) or Rosemary-Almond Salted Caramel Corn (page 29). You could also include heartier party snacks like Sardines and Buttered Saltines (page 22) on your table with the main event. Or, when it's time for a nightcap, try serving a beautiful Cheese Dessert Tray (page 38) to round out the night. Party snacks can usually be prepared ahead of time and don't mind sitting out at room temperature for a little while. They're casual, easygoing, and always welcome.

Sardines and Buttered Saltines
22

Salt-and-Vinegar Potato Peel
Chips with Chive Dip
25

Choose-Your-Own-Adventure
Spiced Nuts
26

Rosemary-Almond Salted
Caramel Corn
29

Extra-Sharp White Cheddar
Seeded Crackers
31

Roasted Winter Fruits
and Cheese Board
33

Charcuterie and
Pickles Platter
36

Cheese Dessert Tray
38

Sardines and Buttered Saltines

Serves 6 to 8

This recipe is like the cool French girl of party snacks—hip yet classic and très chic. Tinned fish makes for ideal impromptu party food because you can store it in your pantry for months and pull it out when you need it. Look for quality sardines packed in 100 percent olive oil.

1 (16-ounce/450 g) package saltine crackers

1 stick (4 ounces/115 g) unsalted butter, melted

4 (4.4-ounce/125 g) tins good-quality sardines in olive oil (try a few different kinds!)

Lemon wedges, for serving

Preheat the oven to 400°F (200°C). Line two sheet pans with parchment paper.

Arrange the crackers in a single layer on the prepared sheet pans. Brush them with melted butter on one side and drizzle any remaining butter over the top. Bake until the edges are golden brown, 7 to 10 minutes, switching racks and rotating the sheets front to back about halfway through.

Meanwhile, open the sardine tins and arrange the fish on a serving platter. You can keep the fish in the tins and offer your guests small forks or toothpicks or you can transfer the fish directly to the platter.

Place the buttered saltines and lemon wedges alongside and serve.

Salt-and-Vinegar Potato Peel Chips with Chive Dip

Serves 6

Three cheers for crispy potatoes! This zero-waste recipe makes use of potato peels that would otherwise be headed for the compost bin—but don't be skeptical, because this party snack is like if a regular potato chip went on vacation to a tiny British coastal village and had a fling with a fisherman. All it takes is a drizzle of olive oil, a quick bake in a hot oven, and a really generous sprinkle of salt. A creamy chive dip alongside makes them feel extra special for a party.

4 russet potatoes, scrubbed

½ cup (120 ml) distilled white vinegar or malt vinegar

Extra-virgin olive oil

Flaky sea salt

½ cup (115 g) sour cream

1 bunch fresh chives, finely chopped

Juice of 1 lemon

Preheat the oven to 400°F (200°C). Line a sheet pan with parchment paper.

Use a vegetable peeler to peel the potatoes. (Set the potatoes aside for another recipe, such as Tiny Samosas with Minty Yogurt Dip, page 75.) Place the peels in a medium bowl, pour in the vinegar, and let soak in the refrigerator for about 20 minutes while the oven preheats.

Drain the potato peels and use a clean kitchen towel to blot them completely dry, which will help them get extra crispy in the oven.

Place the peels on the prepared sheet pan, drizzle with enough olive oil to coat them lightly, and toss well. Sprinkle generously with salt. Spread the peels out into an even layer, spacing them as far apart from one another as possible. Roast, tossing once, until golden brown and crispy, 15 to 20 minutes.

Meanwhile, in a small serving bowl, stir together the sour cream, chives, lemon juice, and ¼ teaspoon salt.

Serve the chips while they're still hot from the oven, with the chive dip alongside.

Choose-Your-Own-Adventure Spiced Nuts

Serves 6

This spiced nut recipe adapts to whatever mood you're in. If you're feeling bright and fresh, try Option 1: the herb garden seasoning blend. Want something spicy? Go for Option 2: the double pepper mix. Or try Option 3: a classic combo of sugar and spice that's reminiscent of the holidays.

Seasoning blend of choice (options follow)

1 large egg white

3 cups (345 g) mixed unroasted nuts, such as walnuts, almonds, and cashews

OPTION 1: HERB GARDEN

½ cup (50 g) freshly grated Parmigiano-Reggiano cheese

2 teaspoons dried oregano

2 teaspoons za'atar

1½ teaspoons fine sea salt

Pinch of red pepper flakes

OPTION 2: DOUBLE PEPPER

¼ cup packed (55 g) brown sugar

2 tablespoons Kashmiri chile powder or 1 to 2 tablespoons of other ground chiles (such as Aleppo pepper)

2 teaspoons fine sea salt

1 teaspoon freshly ground black pepper

OPTION 3: SUGAR AND SPICE

¼ cup packed (55 g) brown sugar

¼ cup (85 g) honey

2 teaspoons fine sea salt

2 teaspoons ground cinnamon

1 teaspoon ground ginger

Pinch of cayenne pepper

Preheat the oven to 325°F (160°C). Line a sheet pan with parchment paper.

Choose a seasoning blend option: In a small bowl, combine all the seasonings and stir well. In a large bowl, whisk the egg white until frothy. Add the nuts and the seasoning blend and mix well. Spread the nuts out on the prepared pan.

Bake, stirring once or twice, until deeply roasted, about 30 minutes. Let cool completely on the pan before serving.

Store the spiced nuts in an airtight container at room temperature for up to 2 weeks.

Rosemary-Almond Salted Caramel Corn

Serves 6

This caramel corn straddles the line between salty and sweet and hits all the right notes. Make sure you splurge on Marcona almonds, which are coated lightly with olive oil and sprinkled with salt.

3 tablespoons extra-virgin olive oil

⅓ cup (75 g) popcorn kernels

1 cup (145 g) Marcona almonds

1 tablespoon fresh rosemary leaves, coarsely chopped

1 stick (4 ounces/115 g) unsalted butter

½ cup packed (105 g) brown sugar

¼ cup (60 ml) maple syrup

3 tablespoons light corn syrup

½ teaspoon fine sea salt

¼ teaspoon baking soda

Flaky sea salt

Preheat the oven to 300°F (150°C). Line a sheet pan with parchment paper.

In a large heavy-bottomed pot, heat the olive oil over medium heat. Add the popcorn kernels and tilt the pot to evenly coat the kernels in the oil. Cover the pot with the lid, leaving it slightly ajar. As soon as you hear the first kernel pop, remove the pot from the heat, shake vigorously (with the lid on!), then let the pot cool down for 1 minute.

Return the pot to medium heat, leaving the lid slightly ajar, and cook until there are 30 seconds or so between pops, about 4 minutes. Transfer the popcorn to a large heatproof bowl, discard any unpopped kernels, and mix in the almonds and rosemary.

In a medium saucepan, combine the butter, brown sugar, maple syrup, and corn syrup. Bring to a boil, stirring to dissolve the sugar. Cook, stirring occasionally, until the mixture reaches 245°F (118°C) on an instant-read thermometer. Remove the pan from the heat and stir in the fine salt and baking soda, which will cause the caramel to bubble. Immediately pour the caramel over the popcorn and stir to coat evenly.

Transfer to the prepared sheet pan, spreading out the popcorn in an even layer. Bake, stirring a few times, until dried and crisp, about 30 minutes. Sprinkle with flaky salt. Let cool completely.

Cooled caramel corn will keep for up to 2 weeks in an airtight container at room temperature.

Extra-Sharp White Cheddar Seeded Crackers

Makes about 45 (1½-inch/4 cm) crackers

There are tons of store-bought options for crackers, of course, but making these seeded cheesy crackers is worth the extra effort. They come out of the oven smelling fantastic, and it's hard to beat that freshly baked, crumbly crunch.

1¼ cups (155 g) all-purpose flour, plus more for rolling

1 cup (115 g) grated extra-sharp white cheddar cheese

½ cup (50 g) freshly grated Parmigiano-Reggiano cheese

½ teaspoon fine sea salt

1 stick (4 ounces/115 g) unsalted butter, cut into small cubes, fridge-cold

1 large egg yolk

2 to 3 tablespoons ice water

1 tablespoon white sesame seeds

1 tablespoon black sesame seeds

1½ teaspoons fennel seeds

1½ teaspoons poppy seeds

In a food processor, combine the flour, cheddar, Parmigiano, and salt. Pulse a few times to mix. Add the butter, egg yolk, and 2 tablespoons ice water. Pulse just until the dough comes together and forms a ball. If the mixture doesn't come together, add 1 tablespoon ice water and continue pulsing until it does.

Divide the dough into 2 equal pieces. On a lightly floured surface, roll each piece into a log about 1½ inches (4 cm) in diameter. Set the logs aside.

Brush away any excess flour or dough bits from the work surface. Place the white sesame seeds, black sesame seeds, fennel seeds, and poppy seeds in a little pile directly on the work surface. Mix them with your fingertips, then spread the mixture out.

Roll each log in the seed mix, pressing gently to adhere the seeds to the outside of the dough. Wrap each log tightly in parchment paper or plastic wrap and refrigerate until thoroughly chilled, at least 2 hours and up to 3 days.

When you're ready to bake the crackers, preheat the oven to 375°F (190°C). Line two sheet pans with parchment paper. Let the dough warm up at room temperature for about 10 minutes, until it's just soft enough to slice without cracking. ➟

Unwrap the dough logs and slice them crosswise into coins ¼ inch (6 mm) thick. Arrange them on the prepared sheet pans. Bake until the crackers are golden brown around the edges, about 20 minutes, switching racks and rotating the sheets front to back halfway through. Transfer the crackers to a wire rack to cool. Serve warm or at room temperature.

Do Ahead Make the dough and chill it in the fridge for up to 3 days or in the freezer for 1 month before baking. The crackers taste best on the day they're baked, but they can be made ahead and stored in an airtight container at room temperature for up to 2 weeks.

GETTING THE PARTY GOING

While parties usually wind down in their own time, sometimes getting things started requires a little extra oomph at the beginning of a party. People can feel a little shy when they are the very first to arrive, but a warm welcome from the host goes a long way. You can't go wrong offering the first guests a drink. If you've already opened a bottle of wine and poured yourself a glass, which I highly encourage (see Hosting Checklist, page 18), then all you need to do is pour a few more glasses for your guests. You could also have a batch cocktail like a Negroni Pitcher (page 264) ready to go, or glasses and ingredients set out so that you can whip up drinks quickly.

If a guest asks how they can help (and you sense they sincerely do want a job to keep busy), put them to work picking herb leaves from stems for garnishing dishes. The best kinds of jobs for guests are the things that can be done at a leisurely pace while enjoying a drink.

A good host also knows the importance of making introductions: Always introduce your first few guests and then, as more people arrive, it will happen naturally. And food is such a wonderful way to bring new people together, so make sure there are some snacks and nibbles ready for everyone.

You can finish up any last-minute items on your to-do list like turning up the music or putting a dish into the oven, but avoid locking yourself in the kitchen in a stressed-out state. One surefire way to get a party off and running is for the host to happily greet and mingle with the guests, drink in hand.

Roasted Winter Fruits and Cheese Board

Serves 6 to 8

A classic cheese board gets a glow-up when you sub roasted fruits for the more traditional fresh fruits. Grapes turn juicy and concentrated in the oven, and apples and pears become tender when cooked briefly with maple syrup and spices, making for a luxurious cheese board that would be ideal for an indulgent celebration like NYE—time to pop the bubbly!

3 pounds (1.4 kg) seedless grapes in clusters

Extra-virgin olive oil

Fine sea salt and freshly ground black pepper

4 tablespoons (½ stick/55 g) unsalted butter

2 large tart green apples, such as Granny Smith, cored and quartered

2 large pears, cored and quartered

3 tablespoons maple syrup

1 cinnamon stick

6 sprigs fresh thyme

1 (12-ounce/340 g) basket ricotta

2 tablespoons honey

1 large wedge (about 6 ounces/170 g) Manchego cheese

6 ounces (170 g) creamy blue cheese, such as Cambozola, Stilton, or Gorgonzola Dolce

Crackers, for serving

Preheat the oven to 450°F (230°C).

Rinse the grapes, pat them dry, and place on a sheet pan. Drizzle generously with olive oil and sprinkle with salt and pepper. Roast, turning the clusters halfway through, until the grapes look plumped and some have burst, about 10 minutes. Let cool on the pan and lower the oven temperature to 400°F (200°C).

In a Dutch oven or heavy-bottomed pot with a lid, melt the butter over medium-high heat. Add the apples and pears and cook, without stirring, until light golden brown on the undersides, about 5 minutes. Add the maple syrup, cinnamon stick, thyme, and a pinch of salt. Cover and transfer to the oven to continue cooking until the fruits are tender when poked with a fork, about 20 minutes.

Arrange the roasted grapes, apples, and pears on a serving platter. Add the ricotta to the platter and drizzle it with the honey. Nestle the Manchego wedge among the fruits and cut a few thin slices from it. Last, find a spot for the blue cheese. Serve with crackers.

HOW TO STYLE A CHEESE BOARD LIKE A PRO

1   **Anchor the board with the cheeses:** If there are three cheeses, arrange them in a triangle (ideally not equilateral!) to anchor the board and create a solid foundation. Two cheeses look best on opposite sides of the board, but do your best to avoid aligning them. For four or more cheeses, distribute them evenly around the board.

2   **Provide cheese knives:** If possible, each cheese gets its own knife. Hard cheeses need sharp blades, and soft, spreadable cheeses are happy with regular table knives.

3   **Fill in the gaps:** Use a variety of complementary components to fill in the empty spaces on the board around the cheeses. Aim for a balanced mix of fresh fruit (grape clusters, cherries, berries of all kinds), dried fruit, nuts, olives and pickles, and crackers or bread.

4   **Embrace asymmetry:** Your goal is for the board to look perfectly imperfect. But making something look effortlessly styled takes effort. Nudge elements out of alignment. Let ingredients fall and cascade where they will. Break the border frame of the board by allowing ingredients to peek over the edge. Try to embrace the beautiful asymmetry of the natural world.

Charcuterie and Pickles Platter

Serves 8 generously

A party snack platter for your favorite meat-eating guests. Choose the finest charcuterie and pickles you can afford. The exact varieties don't matter so much—for example, you can swap out spicy soppressata for any cured meat you love. A certain magic happens when you combine tart pickled vegetables and charcuterie. The acidity of the pickles slices right through the richness of the meat.

4 ounces (115 g) 'nduja

6 ounces (170 g) thinly sliced prosciutto, at room temperature

1 whole soppressata

1 whole finocchiona

1 (6-ounce/170 g) jar pickled peppers

1 (12-ounce/340 g) jar cornichons

1 (8-ounce/225 g) jar mixed pickled vegetables

1 (6-ounce/170 g) jar marinated artichoke hearts

3 pounds (1.4 kg) seedless grapes, cut into clusters

Crackers or bread, for serving

Place the 'nduja on a small plate or bowl and set it on a large serving platter. Drape the prosciutto in billowy folds in a nearby corner or edge of the platter. Use a sharp knife to cut the soppressata and the finocchiona into very thin slices and arrange them in the other two corners.

Drain the pickled peppers, cornichons, mixed pickled vegetables, and artichoke hearts and place them in separate little dishes or piles on the platter.

Nestle the grape clusters among the pickles and charcuterie. Stack and layer the crackers or bread around everything.

Put a blunt-nosed knife near the 'nduja for spreading on crackers or bread. Toothpicks or short wooden skewers are also helpful for spearing the pickles. Serve.

Cheese Dessert Tray

Serves 8 generously

Is this party snack savory or sweet? Hard to say, but one thing's for sure: Everyone can find something to love on this gorgeous tray, whether it's the sliced juicy figs, glistening warmed olives, deep-red cherry jam, or lush creamy cheeses and honey.

7 ounces (200 g) La Tur cheese or other soft Italian cheese

1 large wedge (about 6 ounces/170 g) creamy blue cheese, such as Cambozola, Stilton, or Gorgonzola Dolce

1 large wedge (about 6 ounces/170 g) Parmigiano-Reggiano cheese

½ cup (160 g) sour cherry jam

1 basket ripe figs

½ cup (170 g) honey

MARINATED OLIVES

1 teaspoon cumin seeds

1 dried chile de arbol

3 tablespoons extra-virgin olive oil

1 garlic clove, smashed to crack it open and peeled

3 strips lemon zest, peeled with a vegetable peeler

1 teaspoon fennel seeds

2 cups (360 g) olives with pits, rinsed and drained

Crackers or bread, for serving

About 1 hour before serving, remove the cheeses from the refrigerator and let them warm up at room temperature.

Place the three cheeses in a triangle (either equilateral or isosceles) on a large serving platter or board. Supply a separate serving utensil for each cheese—a blunt-nosed knife is ideal for spreading the La Tur, a small knife for the creamy blue, and a pointy wedge-like knife for breaking off little hunks of the Parmigiano. Leave the La Tur and creamy blue for your guests to make the first cuts, but do get the Parmigiano started by wedging the knife into the cheese and breaking off some large crumbles. Spoon the jam into a small bowl, set a little serving spoon in it, and place near the La Tur cheese.

Cut the figs into wedges and arrange them in one area on the platter, leaning them up against one another in a few places. Spoon the honey into a small bowl and set it near the figs, with a honey twirler for serving.

Make the marinated olives: In a small dry saucepan, toast the cumin seeds and chile de arbol over medium-low heat until fragrant, 1 to 2 minutes. Add the olive oil, garlic, lemon zest strips, fennel seeds, and olives. Turn the heat down to low and cook, stirring often, until the olives are warmed through, about 5 minutes.

Transfer to a small serving dish and set it on the platter, with an empty small bowl alongside for the olive pits.

Nestle the crackers or bread in stacks among everything. Serve.

HOW TO STORE CHEESES

Having a party is a wonderful excuse to buy a few different cheeses that you usually wouldn't buy for just yourself on a regular day. Maybe you choose your favorite ultracreamy cheese that you know everyone will love. Or perhaps you try some new-to-you cheeses. No matter what, you'll want to store the cheeses properly in your fridge so that they taste their best for the party—and any leftover pieces stay fresh until you've enjoyed every last morsel. The best spot in the fridge for cheese is the pull-out vegetable crisper drawer, because it has a steady cool temperature and humidity level; other fridge zones can fluctuate when the doors open and a gust of warm air enters. Here's what to do for each type of cheese:

Fresh cheeses in water or brine (like mozzarella or feta): Store in the original packaging and replace the water with cool tap water every few days, making sure the cheese is fully submerged.

Soft, spreadable cheeses (like La Tur, Brie, or goat cheese): Place in a clean food storage container and cover tightly with a lid.

Semi-hard cheeses (like Gruyère or cheddar): Wrap with plastic wrap or reusable food wrap.

Aged hard cheeses (like Parmigiano-Reggiano): Wrap first with parchment paper and then with plastic wrap or reusable food wrap.

Light-Lift Parties

Not all parties need to be complicated affairs that are planned weeks or months in advance. Those are super special, of course, but what about when you don't have the time to grocery shop, prep, and cook? Sometimes you want to gather with the people you love at a moment's notice. Or, realistically, it's Friday morning and you're at work daydreaming about hosting a little party later that same day. That's the perfect opportunity for a light-lift party! A light-lift party is when you spend minutes instead of hours getting the food ready. It's when you swing by your favorite pizza place on the way home from the office but also toss together an Extraordinary Green Leafy Salad (page 117) in your kitchen. A light-lift brunch might include bacon and a monochrome red fruits salad you made, plus a pink box of jumbo doughnuts. The effort you put in is low, but the rewards are high. After all, parties are really all about spending time with friends and the people you love.

RESTAURANT SHOPPING

You may have noticed that some of the best places to eat also offer foods and packaged products that you can take home. They might sell tins of sardines or bottles of olive oil that they import and use to cook with in the restaurant. Or they might make huge batches of granola, pack it into bags, and offer those. Maybe you've seen house-made pickles, vinegar, and even chocolates. These goods aren't always displayed prominently (or at all in some restaurants). When a restaurant doesn't have an obvious selection to choose from, you just need to be a little creative. Would your favorite pizza spot sell you a ball of dough? Can you talk that Lebanese restaurant you frequent into letting you buy a pint of their exceptional hummus? Use these ingredients to help you easily put together a menu for a light-lift party. For example, serve that

hummus with an assortment of radishes, sliced fennel, carrot sticks, and Persian cucumber spears for dipping, plus some juicy ripe figs and manouri cheese on the side. Call it "restaurant shopping" and think of the foods you buy as decked-out groceries. They're supercharged and ready for the spotlight at home.

SAMPLE LIGHT-LIFT PARTY MENUS

COZY NIGHT IN

- **Extraordinary Green Leafy Salad (page 117)**
- **Pizza ordered from your favorite place and kept warm in a 200°F (90°C) oven**
- **Store-bought ice cream, chocolate sauce, and caramel sauce for sundaes**

COLLEGE SUSHI DINNER ON A SLIGHTLY BIGGER BUDGET

- **Sake bombs**
- **Frozen edamame, boiled briefly in generously salted water, then drained and drizzled with Japanese BBQ sauce**
- **Assorted sushi rolls, arranged on your fanciest platter**
- **Matcha Kit Kats**
- **A pot of green tea**

STEAMY DUMPLINGS FOR A CHILLY NIGHT

- **Frozen dumplings, boiled or steamed**
- **Good-quality chicken broth, heated to a simmer, then poured into warmed bowls**
- **Garnishes:** a jar of chili crisp, thinly sliced scallions, fresh cilantro leaves

Serve the cooked dumplings in the broth and garnish as you like.

PERSONAL PIZZA PARTY

- **One 28-ounce (794 g) can whole, peeled tomatoes**

- **Restaurant-bought pizza dough**

- **All the toppings:** pepperoni, Calabrian chile peppers, fresh mozzarella, basil, pineapple, and so on

Place a sheet pan or pizza stone in your oven and preheat as high as it will go. Make the simplest and best sauce: Put the tomatoes and the juices from their can in a blender, add a few pinches of fine sea salt and a glug of extra-virgin olive oil, and blend on high speed until smooth. Take turns stretching out the dough on the backs of your hands and then everyone makes their own personal pizza.

BRUNCH

- **Your favorite selection of doughnuts**

- **Bacon, placed in a single layer on a foil-lined sheet pan and cooked in a 450°F (230°C) oven until browned and crisp**

- **Monochrome fruit salad:** Try plums, strawberries, raspberries, and cherries

SUNDAY MORNING

- **Bagels bought from the fanciest spot in town**

- **Cream cheese with chopped chives mixed in**

- **Smoked salmon**

- **Garnishes:** thickly sliced tomatoes, thinly sliced red onion, and capers

Starters

A good starter dish kicks off the rest of the menu in an intentional and fun way. You can't go wrong with any of these recipes, but keep in mind that the starter should flow with the other dishes you're planning to serve. Aim for complementary flavors and contrasting textures in your whole menu. For example, a crunchy fried starter like Saffron Arancini (page 79) is a terrific opening act to a meal that includes a nonfried, creamy dish such as Pasta Carbonara (page 191). The best starters are pleasantly salty and bold—all the better to get things going with a bang.

Edamame on Ice with
Black Vinegar Mignonette
44

Homemade Tortillas
and Mango Salsa
47

Turmeric- and Beet-Pickled
Deviled Eggs
49

Brunch Scotch Eggs
53

Tuna Niçoise Tartines
55

Jamón and Fig Toasts
59

Brown Butter Roasted
Radish Toasts
60

Gluten-Free Seeded Bread with
Smoked Salmon Spread
62

Gorgonzola-Prosciutto
Toasties
65

Asparagus Agrodolce
Cigars
66

Bavarian-Style
Soft Pretzels
69

Broiled Bratwurst Bites
71

Spicy Chicken Wings
with Apricot-Honey-
Chile Sauce
73

Tiny Samosas with
Minty Yogurt Dip
75

Saffron Arancini
79

Edamame on Ice with Black Vinegar Mignonette

Serves 4

Serving oysters on the half shell at a party is festive and glamorous, but what if you swap out the oysters and instead give the same VIP treatment to edamame in their pods? The result is unexpectedly delightful. Look no further for something to impress your vegan guests!

Fine sea salt

1 pound (450 g) frozen edamame in the pod

1 teaspoon Sichuan peppercorns

1 large or 2 small shallots, minced

⅓ cup (80 ml) black vinegar

2 teaspoons chili crisp

Ice cubes

Bring a large pot of generously salted water to a boil. Add the edamame and cook until the pods are vibrantly green and the beans inside are tender, 3 to 5 minutes. Drain well.

Transfer the cooked edamame to a container and refrigerate until completely chilled, at least 2 hours and up to 3 days.

In a small dry skillet, toast the Sichuan peppercorns over medium heat, shaking the pan often, until fragrant, 2 to 4 minutes. Transfer the toasted peppercorns to a spice grinder or a mortar and grind to a powder.

In a jar, combine the shallots, vinegar, chili crisp, and ground Sichuan peppercorns. Cover and chill for at least 30 minutes.

Fill a food processor about halfway with ice cubes and pulse until the ice is the size of pebbles. Store the pebble ice in the freezer until you need it.

When you're ready to serve, fold a paper towel and place it in the middle of a serving platter with a lip or in a shallow serving bowl (this will prevent the ice from sliding around). Make a bed of the pebble ice on top of the paper towel in the serving dish. Place the edamame directly on the bed of ice and nestle the jar of black vinegar mignonette into the ice to keep it well chilled.

Do Ahead Cook the edamame, drain, and refrigerate for up to 3 days. The mignonette can also be made up to 3 days ahead and kept in the fridge. Instead of making pebble ice, you can opt for the shortcut of store-bought crushed ice.

Homemade Tortillas and Mango Salsa

Serves 6 to 8

Everyone has been to a party where there's chips and salsa on the table—it's a reliable starter, if a bit expected. This recipe is a variation on chips and salsa that's anything but boring. The juicy, refreshing mango salsa is laced with the zing of Tajín seasoning and fresh jalapeño. And instead of crunchy chips, how about a stack of palm-size soft tortillas made from blue corn masa harina? Making tortillas sounds involved but is actually quick and satisfying, and once you've tasted a homemade tortilla that's still warm from the pan, it's pretty hard to go back to the plastic-wrapped store-bought version. You can prepare the mango salsa ahead of time, but try to serve the tortillas soon after cooking them, when they're still pliable and warm.

MANGO SALSA

¼ cup (40 g) finely chopped white onion

Finely grated zest of 2 limes

¼ cup (60 ml) fresh lime juice

Fine sea salt

2 large mangoes

½ small jalapeño, seeded and minced

½ cup (10 g) fresh cilantro leaves, chopped

½ teaspoon Tajín seasoning

TORTILLAS

1 cup (115 g) blue corn masa harina

1 cup (125 g) all-purpose flour

1 teaspoon baking powder

1 teaspoon fine sea salt

5 tablespoons (65 g) lard

1 cup (240 ml) hot water

Vegetable oil, for the pan

Make the mango salsa: In a medium bowl, combine the onion, lime zest, lime juice, and a pinch of salt. Let rest at room temperature to mellow the sharpness of the onion, about 5 minutes.

Stand one mango up on its stem end and cut down one side, just beyond where you think the oblong pit in the center might be. If the knife meets the pit, just move the blade away from the center of the fruit to cut around the pit. Repeat with the other sides, then with the second mango. Cut each side piece in a crosshatch pattern, cutting through the fruit but not all the way through the skin. Press the skin side inward to invert each mango piece so that the little squares pop out like a porcupine's quills. Cut the fruit away from the skin. ⟶

Add the mango pieces, jalapeño, and cilantro to the bowl with the onion and gently mix. Sprinkle with the Tajín seasoning. Cover and refrigerate the mango salsa until ready to serve.

Make the tortillas: In a medium bowl, stir together the masa harina, flour, baking powder, and salt. Mix in the lard, using your fingertips to rub it into the flour mixture until there are no pieces larger than a pea. Pour in the hot water and stir until well combined, then knead the dough for 3 to 5 minutes. Divide the dough into 12 equal portions and roll into balls. Cover them with a clean kitchen towel and let rest at room temperature for 30 minutes.

Using a tortilla press or a rolling pin, flatten each ball to a 4- to 5-inch (10 to 12.5 cm) round. (Alternatively, you can press down on the ball with a pie plate. And if you have a glass pie plate, even better because you can actually see how big/thin the tortilla is getting.)

Heat a lightly oiled cast-iron skillet over medium heat for 2 minutes. Working with one tortilla at a time, place it in the skillet and cook until puffed and golden brown in a few places on the first side, about 1 minute. Flip and cook on the second side for another 1 minute. Wrap the cooked tortilla in a clean kitchen towel to keep it soft while you cook the remaining tortillas.

Serve the chilled mango salsa with the warm tortillas.

Do Ahead Make the mango salsa up to 2 days before the party. Cook the tortillas the day of the party. To reheat them gently, stack them, wrap in foil, and warm in a 200°F (90°C) oven for 5 minutes before serving.

Turmeric- and Beet-Pickled Deviled Eggs

Serves 6 to 8

Here's a new take on a retro dish. These deviled eggs are dyed either yellow from turmeric or red from beets, and they're lightly pickled in a vinegar bath. The pickling liquid helps tighten the texture of the egg whites a little bit and it also sets the color. You could of course make only one color, if you prefer, but they look so cheerful served together on the same platter, like pops of colorful confetti.

12 large eggs

1½ cups (360 ml) apple cider vinegar

1½ cups (360 ml) water

2 tablespoons sugar

Fine sea salt

2 teaspoons ground turmeric

1 large red beet, peeled and coarsely grated

1½ teaspoons yellow mustard

1 teaspoon yellow curry paste

6 tablespoons (85 g) mayonnaise

1 tablespoon tomato paste

Pinch of smoked paprika

Snipped chives, for garnish

Set up a bowl of ice and water. Bring a medium stainless-steel pot of water to a boil. Carefully lower in the eggs, adjust the heat so that the water simmers gently, and cook for exactly 8 minutes. Transfer the cooked eggs to the bowl of ice water and let cool for 2 minutes, then crack and peel away the shells.

In one 1-quart (1 L) jar, stir together ¾ cup (180 ml) of the vinegar, ¾ cup (180 ml) of the water, 1 tablespoon of the sugar, 1 teaspoon salt, and the turmeric.

In another 1-quart (1 L) jar, stir together the remaining vinegar, water, and sugar, plus 1 teaspoon salt and the grated beet.

Place 6 peeled eggs in each jar, cover, and refrigerate for at least 3 hours.

Use a slotted spoon to remove the pickled eggs from the turmeric and beet brines, keeping the two colors separate and reserving the brines. Cut the eggs in half lengthwise and carefully scoop the yolks into two bowls. Mash the yolks with a fork. To one bowl, mix in the mustard, curry paste, 3 tablespoons of the mayonnaise, and 1 tablespoon of the turmeric pickling brine. To the other bowl of yolks, mix in the tomato paste, the smoked paprika, the remaining 3 tablespoons mayonnaise, and 1 tablespoon of the beet pickling brine.

Spoon or pipe the turmeric yolk mixture into the yellow-dyed egg whites, and spoon or pipe the beet yolk mixture into the pink-dyed egg whites. Arrange them all on a platter, sprinkle with chives, and serve.

Do Ahead Up to 1 week ahead, boil and peel the eggs and place them in their jars to soak in the colorful liquid. Up to 24 hours before the party, continue with the recipe to finish the deviled eggs and chill them in the fridge until ready to serve.

Brunch Scotch Eggs

Serves 6 to 8

Scotch eggs are soft-boiled eggs that get swaddled in ground meat, coated in bread crumbs, and fried until satisfyingly crispy. They are a gastropub staple in the UK, although their roots likely trace back to Indo-Persian koftas. You'll find that these are a great conversation starter at a party because many guests will be surprised to see that the crunchy exterior breaks open to reveal a perfectly jammy egg yolk. Traditionally, Scotch eggs are eaten at bars or on picnics, but this version leans into the breakfast theme—the eggs are wrapped with breakfast sausage and coated with Chex cereal—and would be terrific served at a brunch party.

10 large eggs

1 cup (125 g) all-purpose flour

1 cup (55 g) panko bread crumbs

1 cup (27 g) Rice Chex or Corn Chex cereal, crushed to crumbs

14 ounces (400 g) fresh breakfast sausage, casings removed

1½ quarts (1.4 L) vegetable oil, for frying

English mustard, such as Colman's, for serving

Pickles or cornichons, for serving

Set up a bowl of ice and water. Bring a medium saucepan of water to a boil. Carefully lower in 8 of the eggs, adjust the heat so that the water simmers gently, and cook for exactly 6 minutes. Transfer the cooked eggs to the ice water and let cool for 2 minutes, then crack and peel away the shells.

Place the flour in a shallow bowl and beat the remaining 2 eggs in another shallow bowl. In a third shallow bowl, combine the panko and crushed cereal.

Divide the sausage into 8 equal portions. Press one portion into a thin patty in your palm, then wrap it around one of the boiled eggs, fully encasing the egg with a thin layer of sausage. Repeat to wrap the remaining eggs.

Pour 2 inches (5 cm) vegetable oil into a deep pot and heat to 350°F (177°C) on an instant-read thermometer. Set a wire rack or clean brown paper bags on a sheet pan.

Roll each egg in the flour, then dunk in the beaten egg, and finally dredge in the panko-cereal mixture, pressing gently to adhere the crumbs to the sausage. →

Working in two batches, fry the rolled eggs, stirring occasionally, until crisp and golden brown all over, about 5 minutes. Transfer to the prepared sheet pan and continue frying the remaining rolled eggs.

Serve hot with mustard and pickles.

Do Ahead You can get ahead by boiling the eggs, peeling them, and encasing them in the sausage meat. Keep them in the fridge for up to 3 days. Dredge and fry them just before serving so they're piping hot and crisp.

Variation

GLUTEN-FREE SCOTCH EGGS

Use a gluten-free flour instead of all-purpose and choose gluten-free panko. Both Rice Chex and Corn Chex are already gluten-free.

Tuna Niçoise Tartines

Serves 8

Salad isn't always the easiest food to eat at a party because it requires a fork and two free hands. But when you're looking for a veggie-forward dish or the balanced flavors of your favorite salad, try transforming salad into a party-friendly two-bite toast, like this take on a tuna Niçoise. Plus, unlike tender greens that quickly wilt when sitting out on the table, the hearty radicchio and endive stand up well to the garlicky vinaigrette.

Fine sea salt

6 ounces (170 g) haricots verts, stem ends trimmed (you can leave their little tails on)

2 small garlic cloves, crushed to a paste, plus 2 large garlic cloves, peeled but whole

¼ cup (60 ml) fresh lemon juice

2 teaspoons red wine vinegar

Freshly ground black pepper

Dijon mustard

6 tablespoons (90 ml) extra-virgin olive oil, plus more for brushing/drizzling

1 small head radicchio, torn into bite-size leaves

3 or 4 Belgian endives, separated into individual leaves

1 loaf country-style bread

4 soft-boiled eggs (see Note), peeled, cut into wedges, and sprinkled with flaky salt

2 (5-ounce/140 g) cans tuna in olive oil, drained and flaked

½ cup (65 g) pitted Niçoise olives

Bring a wide skillet of salted water to a boil. Add the haricots verts and cook until bright green and tender but still a little crunchy, about 1½ minutes. Drain. Set aside.

In a large bowl, combine the garlic paste, lemon juice, vinegar, ¼ teaspoon fine sea salt, and lots of pepper. Dip the tines of a clean fork into a mustard jar. When you lift the fork, a small amount of mustard should cling to the tines. Dunk the fork into the lemon juice mixture and stir to incorporate. Pour in the olive oil and stir until emulsified. Add the radicchio and endive leaves to the bowl and use your hands to toss them in the vinaigrette. Set aside.

Preheat the oven to 375°F (190°C). ⟶

Cut the bread into slices ¼ inch (6 mm) thick and then cut each slice into individual tartines—they should be somewhere between 2 and 3 inches (5 and 7.5 cm) long and with crust on only one side at most. Brush or drizzle with olive oil and place close together like puzzle pieces on two sheet pans.

Bake until just barely toasted and crisp, about 5 minutes. As soon as you remove the toasts from the oven, while they are still hot, rub them on one side with the large garlic cloves, gently grating the garlic on the rough surface of the toast.

Arrange the toasts on a serving platter and top them with the dressed leaves, haricots verts, eggs, tuna, and olives.

Note To soft-boil the eggs, follow the first step of Brunch Scotch Eggs (page 53), but cook these eggs for 7 minutes for a slightly firmer set as these eggs don't get cooked further in hot oil.

Do Ahead Cook the haricots verts, drain well, and refrigerate for up to 3 days. The eggs can be soft-boiled and refrigerated up to 3 days ahead, too. You can make the vinaigrette up to 5 days ahead, but don't dress the leaves with it until just before serving. The garlic toasts should be made just before serving.

Jamón and Fig Toasts

Serves 4 to 6

Figs appear twice in this recipe—as jam that's spread on the garlic-rubbed toast and then again as fresh wedges on top, nestled among sliced Manchego cheese and dry-cured Spanish jamón. Make this starter during summertime, when juicy figs are available in farmers' markets.

1 baguette

Extra-virgin olive oil

1 or 2 garlic cloves, peeled but whole

1 (8-ounce/225 g) jar fig jam

6 ounces (170 g) thinly sliced jamón ibérico or prosciutto

3 ounces (85 g) young Manchego cheese, thinly shaved

12 fresh figs, cut lengthwise into wedges

Honey, for drizzling

Preheat the oven to 375°F (190°C).

Cut the baguette on a diagonal into slices that are somewhere between ¼ inch (6 mm) and ½ inch (1.3 cm) thick. Place them on a sheet pan and generously brush with olive oil on both sides. Toast in the oven, flipping halfway through, until golden brown and crisp around the edges but still a little soft and tender in the middle, 5 to 8 minutes.

As soon as the toasts come out of the oven, while they are still hot, rub one side of each slice with garlic. The rough surface of the toast will act like a fine grater, depositing a little bit of garlic on each toast. Keep the toasts with their garlicky side facing up.

Spread a thin layer of jam on each toast. Drape a piece of jamón on each toast, letting it fold on itself in a few places so that it looks billowy and beautiful. Top with a shaving or two of Manchego and a wedge of fresh fig. Drizzle lightly with honey and serve.

Do Ahead You can make the baguette toasts the morning of your party. Remember to rub them with garlic while they're still hot from the oven. Store them, uncovered, at room temperature.

Brown Butter Roasted Radish Toasts

Serves 4 to 6

Radish and salted butter are a match made in heaven. The bracing crunch of radish pairs beautifully with the rich creaminess of butter, and a hint of salt heightens all the flavors. The simple and classic French snack of raw radishes served with smooth, room-temp butter is the inspiration for this recipe. But the twist here is that the radishes are drizzled with melted butter and roasted until tender with only the tiniest bit of crunch, sort of like al dente pasta. To make this starter a little more party-friendly, the radishes are served on top of toasts smeared with herbed goat cheese.

2 bunches radishes (any kind)

4 tablespoons (½ stick/55 g) unsalted butter, melted

Fine sea salt

8 slices country-style bread

1 garlic clove, peeled but whole

2 ounces (55 g) herbed goat cheese

¼ cup (5 g) fresh chervil or flat-leaf parsley, torn or snipped into small sprigs

Lemon wedges, for squeezing

Freshly ground black pepper

Preheat the oven to 425°F (220°C).

Trim the radishes, leaving a little bit of the leafy green top if it looks perky and fresh. Cut each radish lengthwise into quarters and place them all on a sheet pan. Drizzle with the melted butter and sprinkle with salt. Roast, stirring once, until mostly tender with still a little bit of crunch, about 15 minutes.

Meanwhile, toast the bread in a toaster. As each slice finishes toasting, while it's still warm, rub the garlic clove across both sides. (Alternatively, you can toast the bread under the broiler once the radishes are finished.)

Brush the toasts with any browned butter from the sheet pan. Cut the toasts into smaller pieces, spread some herbed goat cheese on each piece, and spoon a few roasted radish wedges on top. Sprinkle with the chervil, squeeze a little lemon juice over the radishes, grind some pepper on top, and serve warm.

Do Ahead Roast the radishes up to 3 days ahead and store, covered, in the fridge. Make sure to keep any browned butter that ends up on the sheet pan and use it to brush on the toasts when you make them!

Gluten-Free Seeded Bread with Smoked Salmon Spread

Serves 6 to 8

This gluten-free bread is made from a mixture of chopped nuts, seeds, and dried fruits and bound together with eggs and oil. The loaf is dense (in the best way) and wonderful as a base for smoked salmon spread. The bread-making process is as easy as stirring all the ingredients together in one bowl, and baking it will make your kitchen smell heavenly. But if you're not up for homemade bread, you can absolutely sub store-bought bread (gluten-free or not).

BREAD

4 large eggs

1 cup (135 g) pistachios, toasted and chopped

1 cup (115 g) walnuts, toasted and chopped

1 cup (140 g) almonds, toasted and chopped

¾ cup (85 g) dried cranberries

¼ cup (35 g) dried apricots, finely chopped

6 tablespoons (55 g) white sesame seeds

6 tablespoons (55 g) black sesame seeds

¼ cup (60 ml) extra-virgin olive oil

1½ teaspoons fine sea salt

SALMON SPREAD

8 ounces (225 g) full-fat cream cheese

4 ounces (115 g) smoked salmon, chopped

1 bunch fresh chives, finely chopped

1½ tablespoons everything bagel seasoning

Make the bread: Preheat the oven to 350ºF (180ºC). Line an 8½ by 4½-inch (21 by 11 cm) loaf pan with parchment paper.

In a large bowl, whisk the eggs until frothy. Mix in the pistachios, walnuts, almonds, cranberries, apricots, white sesame seeds, black sesame seeds, olive oil, and salt. Transfer to the prepared pan, smooth the top, and bake for 45 minutes, or until golden brown around the edges. Transfer the loaf to a wire rack, remove from the pan and discard the parchment, and let cool completely.

Meanwhile, make the salmon spread: In a medium bowl, stir together the cream cheese, smoked salmon, chives, and everything bagel seasoning. Refrigerate until ready to serve.

Cut the seeded bread into slices ¼ inch (6 mm) thick and toast them. Spoon some salmon spread on each toast and serve.

Do Ahead The baked loaf will keep well, loosely wrapped, at room temperature for up to 3 days. You can also make the salmon spread up to 3 days ahead and refrigerate. When it's time to party, all you need to do is slice, toast, spread, and serve.

10 SIMPLE NEARLY NO-COOK APPETIZERS

1 Thinly sliced prosciutto wrapped around ripe summer melon

2 Basket ricotta drizzled with honey and store-bought crackers

3 Mixed olives warmed in a pan with a splash of olive oil

4 Burrata, cherry tomatoes, and the tiniest fresh basil leaves from the bunch

5 Potato chips served in a pretty bowl (they never disappoint!)

6 Oysters on the half shell with lemon wedges for squeezing

7 Banchan bought from your favorite Korean grocery store

8 Fresh figs cut into quarters, drizzled with crème fraîche, and sprinkled with toasted chopped hazelnuts

9 A crudités plate of all the in-season vegetables at the farmers' market and store-bought dip

10 Best-quality anchovies splashed with sherry vinegar and served with garlic-rubbed toast triangles

Gorgonzola-Prosciutto Toasties

Serves 6 to 8

Who doesn't love grilled cheese sandwiches? These are filled with prosciutto and Gorgonzola Dolce for a deluxe version that feels like it dressed up in black tie but is still casual enough to eat with your hands. They're warm and oozy from the melted cheese (perfect during fall and winter) and so satisfying with a glass of chilled sparkling wine. Sometimes, at the fanciest of parties, you can delight your guests by serving an unexpectedly and decidedly un-fancy dish.

Unsalted butter, at room temperature

12 slices country-style bread (each about ½ inch/1.3 cm thick)

12 slices prosciutto

4 ounces (115 g) Gorgonzola Dolce, at room temperature

¼ cup (5 g) fresh flat-leaf parsley, finely chopped

Spread a generous amount of butter on both sides of the bread slices. Heat a large skillet over medium heat. (If you have two large skillets, heat them both.) Working in batches, place the bread in the skillet and cook until golden brown on one side, 2 to 3 minutes. Use a spatula to transfer the slices to a sheet pan. Continue toasting the buttered bread until you've browned all the slices on one side.

Drape 2 slices of prosciutto across half of the toasts, on the toasted sides. Spread the Gorgonzola on the other half of the toasts, on the toasted sides, and sprinkle with the parsley. Sandwich the toasts together, pressing the prosciutto against the Gorgonzola.

Place as many sandwiches as will fit in the skillet and set a small weight (such as a ramekin or heavy mug) on top of each sandwich. Cook until golden brown, about 1 minute, then flip, reapply the weight, and cook until the other side is golden brown and the cheese has melted a little, 1 to 2 minutes.

Cut each toastie into bite-size triangles and arrange them on a serving platter.

Asparagus Agrodolce Cigars

Serves 8

In Italian, *agrodolce* means "sour-sweet"—two flavors that, when paired together, highlight and bring out the best qualities in each other. Here a sweetened vinegar syrup gets brushed on asparagus spears that are then wrapped in puff pastry, dusted with cheese, and baked. Puff pastry is such a glorious party trick to have up your sleeve. Stash a box of store-bought puff pastry in your freezer—it thaws in a flash and turns puffy and wonderfully flaky in a hot oven. You can use it for all kinds of recipes, starting with these easy asparagus agrodolce cigars.

½ cup (120 ml) apple cider vinegar or red wine vinegar

3 tablespoons sugar

All-purpose flour, for rolling

2 sheets (from one 14-ounce/400 g or 17.3-ounce/490 g package) frozen puff pastry, thawed

36 thick asparagus spears

1 egg, beaten

1 cup (110 g) grated Pecorino Romano cheese

1½ teaspoons dried oregano

¼ teaspoon red pepper flakes

Preheat the oven to 400°F (200°C). Line two sheet pans with parchment paper.

In a small stainless-steel saucepan, combine the vinegar and sugar and simmer over medium-high heat until reduced to a syrup, 8 to 10 minutes. Let cool slightly.

Meanwhile, on a lightly floured surface, roll out each sheet of puff pastry into a 9-inch (23 cm) square. Cut the square into 18 equal strips, each about ½ inch (1.3 cm) wide.

Line up the asparagus in a single layer with the tips all pointed in the same direction on a plate. Brush the vinegar syrup on the asparagus.

Wrap one puff pastry strip in a corkscrew spiral around each asparagus spear by holding the asparagus in one hand and wrapping the puff pastry down the length of it without overlapping the dough. Place the spears on the prepared sheet pans, leaving about 1 inch (2.5 cm) of space between them. Lightly brush the cigars with the beaten egg and sprinkle with the Romano, oregano, and pepper flakes.

Bake until the pastry is golden brown and crisp, 15 to 20 minutes, switching racks and rotating the sheets front to back about halfway through. Serve hot or warm.

Do Ahead Make the sweetened vinegar up to 3 days ahead and store it in an airtight container in the fridge. Up to 2 days ahead, you can wrap the asparagus spears in the puff pastry, place them on a sheet pan (or a plate, if that fits more easily in your fridge), and chill in the refrigerator. On the day of the party, brush and sprinkle the wrapped asparagus just before baking.

MAKING A PLAYLIST

Music enlivens parties of all kinds, and a playlist is one fantastic way to echo the theme or vibe of a party. Putting together a playlist might be something you do well—or it might be a job to assign to your most musically inclined friend. There's always someone in a friend group who has the best taste in music and stays up on all the latest releases. Put them in charge! After all, the best party planners know how important delegation is. Especially for large parties, don't be afraid to delegate tasks so that you can focus your attention on the parts you're best at or that mean the most to you. And if there's nobody obvious to take on the role of DJ, you can always look for public playlists from people you admire (musicians or otherwise) or try streaming auto-generated music based on key words like *dinner party* or whatever seems fitting.

Some great albums for parties:

- *Graceland* by Paul Simon
- *Musas* (Vol. 1 and Vol. 2) by Natalia Lafourcade and Los Macorinos
- *Sunrise* by Surfer Girl
- *Non-Stop: Mexico to Jamaica* by Ozomatli
- *Ritual* by Bay Ledges
- *Contra Los Roboticos Mutantes* by the Spam Allstars
- *Cupid Deluxe* by Blood Orange
- *Days Are Gone* by HAIM
- *Is This It* by The Strokes
- *Body Talk* by Robyn
- *Sound of Silver* by LCD Soundsystem
- *Stop Making Sense (Live)* by Talking Heads
- *Whitney Houston* by Whitney Houston
- *Heard It in a Past Life* by Maggie Rogers
- *Wolfgang Amadeus Phoenix* by Phoenix
- *Rumours* by Fleetwood Mac
- *4* by Beyoncé
- *Butterfly* by Mariah Carey

Bavarian-Style Soft Pretzels

Makes 8 pretzels

These soft pretzels are perfect for a game-day party, or when you have some friends over for beers and you want to really impress them. Making pretzels may sound intimidating, but the dough comes together in one bowl and the yeast really does all the hands-off work—the hardest part is figuring out how to shape the pretzels. (There are tons of videos online if you need a clear visual example!) Two ingredients in the dough make these pretzels extra flavorful: There's a whole can of pilsner beer mixed in, plus some barley malt syrup, which ups the bold flavor of malted toasted grain. Plan ahead for the dough to rise overnight.

½ cup (120 ml) warm water

2 tablespoons barley malt syrup

2 (¼-ounce/7 g) packets active dry yeast

5½ cups (700 g) bread flour, plus more for rolling

1 (12-ounce/360 ml) can pilsner beer

2 tablespoons unsalted butter, at room temperature

1 tablespoon fine sea salt

Vegetable oil

¼ cup (70 g) baking soda

1 large egg

1 tablespoon milk

Flaky sea salt

In the bowl of a stand mixer, combine the water, barley malt syrup, and yeast. Stir to dissolve the syrup, then set aside until the mixture is frothy, about 5 minutes.

Add the flour, beer, butter, and fine salt to the bowl. Snap on the dough hook and mix on low speed until a dough comes together. Increase the speed to medium and knead until smooth, elastic, and slightly sticky, about 7 minutes.

Transfer the dough to a very large oiled bowl, cover, and refrigerate until doubled in size, at least overnight or up to 24 hours.

Line two sheet pans with parchment paper.

On a floured surface, divide the dough into 8 equal portions. Roll each portion into a rope at least 24 inches (61 cm) long. Working with one rope at a time, lift both ends to form a U shape. Twist the ends around each other once, then set them down on top of the fat belly part of the rope and press to adhere the dough. Place the shaped pretzels on the prepared sheets. Cover and let rise in a warm place until puffy, about 30 minutes.

About 15 minutes before the pretzels are done rising, preheat the oven to 450°F (230°C).

In a medium saucepan, bring about 6 cups (1.4 L) water to a boil. Turn on the vent above the stovetop and add the baking soda to the pot. Using a slotted spoon, lower each pretzel into the water and cook for 20 seconds. Flip and cook for another 20 seconds on the other side. Return the dipped pretzels to the sheet pans.

In a small bowl, stir together the egg and milk. Brush the egg wash on the pretzels and sprinkle with flaky salt. Bake until the pretzels are deep brown, 10 to 15 minutes, switching racks and rotating the sheets front to back about halfway through. Let cool slightly on a wire rack and serve warm.

Do Ahead Soft pretzels can be made up to 1 day ahead and stored in an airtight container at room temperature. Before serving, reheat them on a sheet pan in a 200°F (90°C) oven until warmed, 5 to 10 minutes.

Broiled Bratwurst Bites

Serves 6 to 8

Another trick for making foods easier to eat in a standing-room-only party is to serve them in one-bite portions. Pay close attention to the way in which you cut the ingredients. A random chop won't look appetizing, but cutting the bratwurst on the diagonal creates a beautiful shape. Look for small shallots for this recipe because you'll be cutting them in half lengthwise and you want them to stay together and still be bite-size.

2 pounds (910 g) bratwurst

12 small shallots

1 (10-ounce/285 g) jar hot cherry peppers, drained

¼ cup (60 ml) extra-virgin olive oil

Fine sea salt and freshly ground black pepper

Preheat the oven to 425°F (220°C). Put a sheet pan in the oven to heat while you prepare the sausage and vegetables.

Cut the bratwurst crosswise on a diagonal into slices ¾ inch (2 cm) thick and place them in a large bowl. Cut the shallots in half lengthwise, peel away their papery layers, and add to the bowl. Remove the stems from the cherry peppers, cut each pepper in half, and add to the bowl along with the olive oil, a few pinches of salt, and lots of black pepper. Use your hands to gently mix everything until well coated in oil. Transfer to the preheated sheet pan and roast, stirring once or twice, until the sausage pieces are browned and the shallots are tender, about 30 minutes.

Switch the oven to the broiler setting and cook until the sausages are dark brown in a few places, 2 to 3 minutes. Watch the pan carefully and move it as needed to avoid burning.

Serve hot, on skewers, spearing a piece of bratwurst, shallot, and cherry pepper on each skewer.

Spicy Chicken Wings with Apricot-Honey-Chile Sauce

Serves 4 to 6

You can't go wrong serving a beloved classic at a party. These wings are sauced with a sweet-and-sticky mixture of apricot jam, honey, and hot sauce and can be cooked either on the grill or in the oven. If you're planning ahead, you can prep the wings and let them chill in the fridge for up to 2 days before cooking them.

1 tablespoon baking powder

Fine sea salt and freshly ground black pepper

3 pounds (1.4 kg) chicken wings (any combination of wingette, drumette, and tips), patted dry

2 tablespoons extra-virgin olive oil

¾ cup (180 ml) buffalo-style hot sauce, such as Frank's

4 tablespoons (½ stick/55 g) unsalted butter, melted

¼ cup (80 g) apricot jam

2 tablespoons honey

You can grill these wings or cook them in a hot oven. If using an oven, line two sheet pans with foil. (If grilling, no need to line the sheet pans.)

In a large bowl, stir together the baking powder, 1 tablespoon salt, and lots of black pepper. Add the wings and toss to coat. Transfer the wings to the prepared sheet pans and spread them out in a single layer. Let rest at room temperature for 30 minutes or in the refrigerator for up to 2 days.

About 15 minutes before you're ready to cook the wings, heat the oven to 450°F (230°C) or preheat a grill to medium or medium-high.

Drizzle the olive oil over the wings and toss to coat them evenly. Roast or grill, turning halfway through, until golden brown and crisp all over. If you're cooking on a grill, the wings should cook in about 20 minutes, or if in the oven, about 30 minutes.

Meanwhile, in a large bowl, combine the hot sauce, melted butter, jam, honey, and ¼ teaspoon salt. Set aside half of the mixture to serve as a dipping sauce.

If grilling, when the wings are done cooking, brush them with the sauce and continue grilling until the sauce heats through and cooks onto the wings, 1 to 2 minutes. ⟶

If roasting in the oven, when the wings are cooked through, switch the oven to broil. Use tongs to transfer the roasted wings directly to the bowl of sauce. Toss until coated, then return the sauced wings to the sheet pan and cook under the broiler until sizzling and dark brown in spots, about 5 minutes, moving the pan as needed to brown the wings evenly.

Serve hot or warm, with the extra sauce on the side.

Tiny Samosas with Minty Yogurt Dip

Serves 6 to 8

Tiny samosas are ideal party starters because they're small enough to eat in a few bites and they're dippable (in minty yogurt sauce), which is always fun. When you're putting together a menu for your party, look for recipes in Mains (page 138) and Sides and Salads (page 84) that have some of the same spices as these samosas. That's a neat party trick you can use for any menu to create a through line of flavor in the whole meal from start to finish.

SAMOSAS

2 cups (250 g) all-purpose flour

¼ cup (60 ml) plus 2 tablespoons vegetable oil

Fine sea salt

½ cup (120 ml) cold water

1½ pounds (680 g) russet potatoes, peeled and cut into 1-inch (2.5 cm) pieces

1 teaspoon cumin seeds

1 teaspoon black mustard seeds

1 small yellow onion, finely chopped

1 (2-inch/5 cm) piece fresh ginger, peeled and finely grated

2 garlic cloves, finely grated

1 teaspoon garam masala

½ teaspoon ground turmeric

½ cup (75 g) frozen peas

Handful of fresh cilantro leaves, chopped

2 tablespoons fresh lemon juice

MINTY YOGURT DIP

2 cups (40 g) fresh mint leaves

1 cup (20 g) fresh cilantro leaves and tender stems

2 small hot green chiles

1 teaspoon sugar

1 teaspoon cumin seeds

¼ cup (60 ml) fresh lemon juice

1 teaspoon fine sea salt

⅓ cup (85 g) plain whole-milk yogurt

TO FINISH

1 quart (1 L) vegetable oil, for deep-frying

Make the dough: In a medium or large bowl, combine the flour, ¼ cup (60 ml) of the vegetable oil, and ¼ teaspoon salt. Use your fingertips to rub the oil into the flour until the mixture has a mealy texture. Stir in the cold water. Transfer to a clean work surface and knead for 1 minute, then cover with a clean kitchen towel and let rest for 30 minutes.

Meanwhile, bring a large pot of generously salted water to a boil. Add the potatoes and cook until tender when poked with a fork, about 15 minutes. Drain. Use a masher or large fork to smash the potatoes until mostly smooth but still a little chunky. ⟶

In a large skillet, warm the remaining 2 tablespoons vegetable oil over medium-high heat. Add the cumin and black mustard seeds and use a wooden spoon to stir them around in the oil until they are fragrant and toasted, about 1 minute. Add the onion and ¼ teaspoon salt and cook, stirring occasionally, until softened and golden, about 10 minutes. Stir in the ginger, garlic, garam masala, and turmeric and let sizzle for 1 minute. Add the peas and mashed potatoes and cook, stirring often, until well incorporated and heated through, 2 to 3 minutes. Transfer to a bowl, stir in the cilantro and lemon juice, and let cool.

Make the minty yogurt dip: In a high-powered blender, combine the mint, cilantro, green chiles, sugar, cumin seeds, lemon juice, and salt and blend until smooth. Stir the mint mixture into the yogurt, leaving it swirly and not quite completely incorporated. Refrigerate until ready to serve.

To finish: Divide the dough into 20 equal portions about the size of golf balls (about 40 g each) and use your palms to roll each piece into a ball. Cover them with a clean, damp kitchen towel. Working with one ball at a time, and keeping the other pieces covered, use a rolling pin to flatten each ball to a 5-inch (12.5 cm) round. Cut the round straight down the middle into 2 half-moons.

Shape each half-moon into a cone by pinching the flat cut side together. Fill the cone with a heaped 1 tablespoon of the potato mixture and pinch the opening closed to seal the samosa. Repeat to form the other samosas.

Pour 2 inches (5 cm) vegetable oil into a large, heavy-bottomed pot and heat the oil to 350°F (177°C) on an instant-read thermometer. Line a sheet pan with a wire rack or paper towels.

When the oil is ready, carefully lower as many samosas as will fit comfortably without crowding in the pot. Fry until golden brown on the first side, 1 to 2 minutes, then flip and fry on the other side until golden brown, another 1 to 2 minutes. Use a slotted spoon or tongs to transfer to the prepared sheet pan. Continue frying the samosas in batches until you've cooked them all.

Serve the samosas when they're still warm and crispy, but don't stress if they cool down—they're delicious at room temperature, too. Serve the minty yogurt as cold as possible and on the side for dipping.

Do Ahead Prep the filling for the samosas up to 3 days ahead and store it in an airtight container in the fridge. The dip can also be made and refrigerated up to 3 days ahead. Fry the filled samosas the day of the party.

Saffron Arancini

Makes about 16 arancini

Name a better dish than arancini to serve alongside a glass of chilled sparkling white wine. I'll wait! The crispy fried exterior and the salty, cheesy interior are everything you want in a bite. These do take some time to make because you need to cook the rice before shaping the balls, so be sure to plan ahead. But your efforts will be rewarded because what makes arancini perfect for parties is that they are best prepped ahead of time. The balls stay together and are easier to shape when the cooked rice has had a chance to thoroughly chill in the fridge. You can cook the rice up to 3 days before you shape and fry the balls.

3 cups (710 ml) good-quality chicken broth

3 cups (710 ml) water

Fine sea salt

Pinch of saffron threads

3 tablespoons olive oil

1 small yellow onion, finely chopped

1½ cups (300 g) medium-grain risotto rice, such as Arborio, Vialone Nano, or Carnaroli

¼ cup (60 ml) dry white wine (or 1 tablespoon white wine vinegar and 3 tablespoons water)

2 tablespoons unsalted butter

½ cup (50 g) freshly grated Parmigiano-Reggiano cheese

1 orange

1 cup (55 g) panko or regular dried bread crumbs (110 g)

1 teaspoon dried oregano

4 ounces (115 g) mozzarella cheese, cut into ½-inch (1.3 cm) cubes

⅓ cup (85 g) store-bought pesto

1½ quarts (1.4 L) vegetable oil

½ cup (10 g) fresh flat-leaf parsley, finely chopped

In a medium saucepan, bring the broth and water to a simmer. Taste for seasoning, adding ¼ teaspoon of salt at a time until the mixture tastes as salty as soup. Use your fingertips to crumble the saffron and drop it into the broth.

Heat a wide, heavy-bottomed pot over medium heat. Add the olive oil, onion, and ½ teaspoon salt. Cook, stirring frequently, until the onion is softened, about 4 minutes. Stir in the rice and cook for a few minutes, until lightly toasted and fragrant. Pour in the wine and cook until it evaporates. Using a ladle, add about ½ cup (120 ml) of the warm saffron broth to the pot. Cook, stirring occasionally, until the rice has absorbed the liquid and thickened, about 5 minutes. Continue adding the broth ½ cup (120 ml) at a time, letting the rice absorb all the liquid after each addition and stirring often to prevent the rice from sticking. The risotto is done when the rice is tender but retains a slight firmness at its core, like al dente pasta. (You may not need all the broth; on the other hand, if you run out of broth and the risotto isn't done yet, add hot water ½ cup/120 ml at a time until it is.)

Remove the risotto from the heat. Add the butter and Parmigiano. Finely grate the orange over the pot, letting the zest fall into the risotto. Cut the orange in half and squeeze each half over a cupped hand to catch any seeds into the risotto as well. Let rest for 2 to 3 minutes, then stir vigorously until the risotto becomes a little creamier.

Transfer to a parchment-lined sheet pan, spread out evenly, and let cool for about 30 minutes. Cover with plastic and refrigerate until completely chilled, at least 1 hour and preferably longer (as the balls will be easier to shape and will hold together nicely), up to 3 days.

In a wide, shallow bowl, stir together the panko, oregano, and ¼ teaspoon salt.

Scoop 3-tablespoon portions of the chilled risotto, flatten each one into a disk, and place one mozzarella cube and a small spoonful of pesto in the center. Pinch the risotto around the filling and roll the ball between your palms, making sure the filling is well sealed inside. Roll each filled ball in the panko mixture and place them all on a sheet pan. Refrigerate for 30 minutes or freeze for 10 minutes to chill and firm up before frying.

Pour 2 inches (5 cm) vegetable oil into a deep pot and heat the oil to 350°F (177°C) on an instant-read thermometer. Line a sheet pan with a wire rack or clean brown paper bags.

Working in batches, fry the arancini, leaving at least 1 inch (2.5 cm) of space between the balls in the pot, until crisp and golden all over, 4 to 5 minutes. Transfer to the prepared sheet pan and continue frying the remaining arancini. Sprinkle with the chopped parsley and serve hot.

Do Ahead This is a real do-ahead winner because the risotto is actually much easier to shape into balls if it has had plenty of time to chill in the fridge. You can make it up to 3 days ahead. Then shape the arancini and return them to the fridge until you're ready to fry. The best arancini are those served piping hot out of the frying oil, but if you don't want to fry during the party, you can keep arancini hot by placing them on a sheet pan in a 200°F (90°C) oven.

Setting the Table

A party transforms from an idea into a reality the moment you set the table. If you like, you can set the table a day or two before the party. Doing so will probably make you even more excited about what's to come.

TABLECLOTHS

Do you really need a tablecloth? Well, of course you don't need one, but laying down a cloth will add some softness and warmth to the table. That might be exactly what you want if you're hosting a cozy Friends and Family Sunday Supper (page 278) or a party during the cold middle of winter. Light tablecloths with floral prints are perfectly at home for a springtime party, and heavier, darker cloths work well when the party calls for some moody energy. Don't forget to consider tablecloths for outdoor parties, too. You can cover up a public park picnic table with a fresh, clean linen. And, if you think about it, a picnic blanket is sort of like a tablecloth for the ground. Tablecloths need not be fancy. Check garage sales and antique stores for vintage cloths at reasonable prices.

CANDLES

There's one important rule to keep in mind about candles: Only unscented candles are allowed on the table, please! You don't want any scents to clash with the appetizing aromas of the food. Scented candles are lovely in the bedroom and bathroom—and that's where they should stay. In fact, you might consider lighting one in the bathroom before the party starts and letting it burn the whole time. Candles are wonderful because they offer gentle low light. When you have multiple sources of soft light that are at or below eye level, you can literally make a room glow. The low-level part is key for creating the most flattering lighting on faces. A bright overhead light casts harsh shadows downward on your face but a candle brightens from below. If you can, try to have at least a few candles on your table. Tapers, pillars, and tea lights all have their place, and it's totally up to you to decide which you prefer. IKEA sells affordable unscented candles in all shapes and sizes.

PLATES, GLASSES, AND FLATWARE POSITIONS

We've all had that moment of setting a table and wondering, *Wait, which side does the fork go on?* The correct answer is that the fork is placed on the left side of the plate and the knife goes on the right side, with the sharp edge of the blade nearest the plate, for safety. A memory recall trick for this rule is to remember that most people are right-handed and they would want to hold the knife in their right hand. Same goes for the positioning of the glass—above and to the right of the plate, where a right-handed person would naturally reach.

SEATING

It is up to you as the host to decide if you want to assign seating for your guests. You might purposely seat two friends who are new to the friend group next to each other, or you might want to split up couples to encourage them to mingle with others. If making place cards sounds fun to you, try creating them out of something beautiful or creative like images cut from magazines or wall calendars, postcards, and so on.

What happens when you invite eight friends over to your apartment and you have only four chairs? Get creative with the seating! Most people don't have a huge dining table that'll seat twelve comfortably, and making do with what you have is all part of the fun. When there's delicious food and drinks, your guests will not care about the chairs. If you are hosting a large group, you can plan a menu of dishes that are best eaten without a fork while standing—little bites like Extra-Sharp White Cheddar Seeded Crackers (page 31) and a cheese board would be fantastic. Most of the recipes in this book don't require a fork and knife, and the ones that do can be adapted as needed. For example, let's say you'd like to serve Brisket and Harissa Buttered Carrots (page 156), but there won't be room for guests to sit all together around a big table. You can make mini sandwiches; see Brisket Sandwiches (page 158) for the details on how to do it.

PLAN AHEAD

Setting the table is one of the first party planning tasks you can check off your to-do list. The actual making of food and drinks (or, at least, the finishing steps) must happen within hours of your party (see The Art of Serving, page 135, for more about cooking ahead).

Keep in mind that party platters and fancy glassware may have collected some dust between uses. Washing glasses usually takes longer than you think it will, so it's smart to get this job done ahead of time, when you're not in a rush. It can also be a good idea to set aside any serving dishes and serving utensils that you'll need for your menu. If it's helpful to you, label each one with a Post-it note to keep track of which dish is going to hold what food. Seeing all the dishes helps you visualize the whole meal, and you can decide if you like the way everything looks together on the table.

DIY FAUX LINEN TABLECLOTH

If you've ever lusted over those (très expensive!) gorgeous French countryside linen tablecloths, with their nubby texture and perfectly warm neutral color, here's a trick for how you can easily make the best DIY version:

Step 1: All you need is a painter's canvas drop cloth from the hardware store. They are extremely affordable (we're talking less than $10 for a cloth that's 6 by 9 feet/1.8 by 2.7 meters) and they come in a variety of sizes, so choose one that fits your table. If you want to make it look custom, you can cut the drop cloth and then sew the edge to prevent it from fraying. When considering how big your tablecloth should be, know that the distance the cloth drapes off the edge of the table is typically 6 to 8 inches (5 by 20 cm) for casual parties and up to 15 inches (38 cm) for formal events. This is just a rule of thumb, so don't worry too much about sticking closely to it if you find a cool vintage cloth that's a little outside the range.

Step 2: Run the drop cloth through the washing machine and dryer on the highest heat setting at least once—a few laundering cycles will be even better for that vintage look and feel. (It'll also get better with time as you use it, clean it, and use it again.) You can wash the drop cloth with a splash of bleach to lighten the color if you want. The bleach won't turn the cloth pure white; it'll just shift the color slightly lighter to a beautiful neutral that's not quite beige and not quite cream either.

Et voilà! Now you've made a faux linen tablecloth. When your friends ask if you bought it at a market somewhere in the south of France, you can decide how you'll answer that question.

Sides & Salads

Sides and salads are no second fiddle to the main. They're key parts of the menu for parties of all kinds. Take Thanksgiving, for example. We all know the side dishes are secretly (or not so secretly!) the best parts of the meal. Another beauty of side dishes is that they can suit various dietary restrictions—they are usually vegetarian or vegan and often gluten-free, too. When planning your menu, choose sides that complement the other dishes. A good rule of thumb is to have at least one green thing. Next, think about balancing textures and flavors. If your main dish is roasted in the oven, look for a side dish that provides contrast to the golden brown, caramelized flavors—perhaps a crunchy, bright Radish and Avocado Salad (page 122). Having enough food (in terms of quantity) for a party is important, but so, too, is having at least one dish that feels satiating in a comforting way. Something starchy like Toothpick Gnocchi with Oregano Bread Crumbs (page 113) fills people up and helps make the meal feel like a party.

Shoestring Fries Tower and Roasted Garlic Aioli

Serves 6

Go big, big, big! Pile the fries as high as you possibly can for the most dramatic effect. You might think of frying foods at home as an intimidating task (there's the large pot of bubbling hot oil, for one), but the secret here is that french fries—possibly the best fried food—are totally doable! You just need the right prep—the key being soaking the sliced potatoes, which draws out some of the potato starch and helps create that irresistibly crisp texture—as well as a few other helpful tips, like working in batches to fry the potatoes so that they can bob around comfortably in the oil. And you just might find that french fries are extra special when served at a party. All your guests know the lengths you went to, and they're impressed by your efforts.

ROASTED GARLIC AIOLI

1 head garlic

¾ cup (180 ml) extra-virgin olive oil, plus more for drizzling

Fine sea salt

1 large egg yolk

½ lemon

SHOESTRING POTATOES

2 russet potatoes (about 1 pound/ 450 g total)

6 cups (1.4 L) vegetable oil, for frying

Fine sea salt

¼ cup (5 g) fresh flat-leaf parsley, finely chopped, for garnish

Preheat the oven to 400°F (200°C).

Make the roasted garlic aioli: Trim the top ¼ inch (6 mm) or so off the garlic head to expose the cloves. Peel off and discard any of the garlic's loose papery layers that you can easily pull away from the head without breaking the head into individual cloves. Place the garlic head on a piece of foil, drizzle with a little olive oil, sprinkle with salt, and wrap tightly. Roast for 45 minutes.

Unwrap the garlic from the foil, let cool slightly, then squeeze the roasted cloves into a small bowl. Using a fork, smash them to a chunky paste. (Roasted garlic can be made up to 3 days ahead and stored in an airtight container in the refrigerator.)

In a medium bowl, whisk the egg yolk to break it up. While whisking continuously, add a few drops of the olive oil. Whisk until fully incorporated, then add a few more drops of oil. Continue whisking and adding the oil by the drop until the mixture thickens, looks sticky, and pulls away from the sides of the bowl. While whisking, add a little more oil, this time in a very thin and slow stream. Once you've added somewhere between one-third and one-half of the ¾ cup oil, squeeze in a little lemon juice to thin the aioli. Add the remaining oil, still in a very thin and slow stream while whisking continuously. The aioli should be as thick as mayonnaise. Stir the roasted garlic paste into the aioli along with a pinch of salt. Taste and adjust the seasoning, adding more salt and/or lemon juice if you'd like. Transfer the aioli to a small serving bowl or store in an airtight container in the refrigerator for up to 2 days.

Prepare the shoestring potatoes: Using a mandoline or sharp knife, cut the potatoes lengthwise into matchsticks about ⅛ inch (3 mm) thick. Place the potatoes in a large bowl, cover with cold water, and let soak for at least 30 minutes.

About 20 minutes before you're ready to serve, fry the potatoes. Pour 3 inches (7.5 cm) vegetable oil into a large, heavy-bottomed pot. Heat the oil over medium-high heat until it reaches 350°F (177°C) on an instant-read thermometer.

Meanwhile, drain the potatoes from their soaking water and pat thoroughly dry with a clean kitchen towel or paper towels. Blot away as much moisture as possible for the crispiest fries. Line a sheet pan with a wire rack or clean brown paper bags.

When the oil is ready, carefully add about one handful of potatoes and cook, stirring with a slotted spoon a few times, until golden brown and crisp, 3 to 4 minutes. Use the slotted spoon to transfer the fries to the prepared sheet pan (see Note). Sprinkle generously with salt. Repeat to fry the remaining potatoes in batches. (Be careful not to overload the pot with too many potatoes—the very hot oil can bubble up and out.)

To serve, arrange the shoestring fries on a serving platter, piling them up into a tower that's tall and dramatic. Sprinkle with the chopped parsley. Serve as hot and fresh out of the frying oil as you can manage, with the roasted garlic aioli on the side for dipping.

Note You can keep the fries warm on a sheet pan in a 200°F (90°C) oven, but they'll get crunchier the longer they're in there. I think a lukewarm fry with the tiniest bit of bend to it is better than an overly crunchy, hot fry—but you're the host and this is your party, so you get to decide!

Minty Pea Soup with Crème Fraîche Swirl

Serves 6

This soup is the perfect bright moment for a spring day that still has a bit of a chill to it. But it's also as delicious served hot as it is chilled. You can make this soup ahead of time and chill it, and then there's a nice party trick here: Serve your beautiful chilled soup to your guests first, giving you time to work on frying a main dish or putting finishing touches on some other part of the meal. The toppings are what take this soup to the next level: crème fraiche swirled in each bowl, a sprinkling of grated Parmigiano, some fresh lemon zest, and freshly ground black pepper. Garnish with abandon—or simply set out bowls of garnishes and encourage your guests to top their own bowls just how they like.

1 large or 2 small leeks

3 tablespoons unsalted butter

2 garlic cloves, thinly sliced

Fine sea salt

¼ cup (60 ml) white wine

4 cups (950 ml) good-quality chicken broth

8 ounces (225 g) frozen peas

2 ounces (55 g) fresh baby spinach (about 3 cups)

1 cup (20 g) fresh mint leaves

Crème fraiche

Grated Parmigiano-Reggiano cheese

Finely grated zest of 1 lemon

Freshly ground black pepper

Trim away any dark green parts of the leek, then slice the white and light-green parts into thin rounds. Drop them into a large bowl of cool water, swish with your fingers to dislodge any trapped dirt, and let soak for a few minutes.

In a large pot, melt the butter over medium-high heat. Lift the leeks out of the bowl (leaving behind any dirt at the bottom of the bowl) and add them to the pot. Cook, stirring occasionally, until softened, about 5 minutes. Add the garlic and ½ teaspoon salt and continue cooking, stirring often, for 2 minutes.

Add the wine and broth and bring to a boil over high heat. Once the broth is bubbling vigorously, stir in the peas, spinach, and mint. Let cook for 1 minute, then remove the pot from the heat.

Use an immersion blender (or carefully transfer the soup to a high-powered blender) and puree until very smooth. Taste and season with salt. If serving hot, divide the soup among serving bowls and garnish each with a big spoonful of crème fraîche, a sprinkling of grated Parmigiano, a pinch of lemon zest, and a few grinds of pepper. If you prefer to serve the soup chilled, which is lovely on a warm day, transfer the soup to an airtight container, refrigerate until cold, and add the garnishes just before serving.

5 WAYS WITH A GOOD LOAF OF BREAD

1   **The Good Ol' Breadbasket (or Dish):** Cut a loaf into thick slices, place in an ovenproof dish, and warm in a 200°F (90°C) oven for about 5 minutes. Serve straight out of the oven with the fanciest salted butter you can afford, at room temperature so it's easy to spread. Set in the middle of the table and watch as everyone eagerly reaches for a piece.

2   **Toast with Soup:** Toast slices of bread, butter each piece or drizzle with olive oil, and sprinkle with flaky salt. Serve alongside soup to make the dish a little more filling (or to stretch a meal to feed a few extra unexpected guests). Try the Minty Pea Soup with Crème Fraîche Swirl (pictured at right).

3   **Out-of-This-World Garlic Bread:** In a small bowl, stir together ½ cup (1 stick/115 g) melted unsalted butter, 6 finely grated garlic cloves, a handful of grated Parmigiano-Reggiano cheese, another handful of finely chopped flat-leaf parsley, and 2 big pinches of salt. Thickly slice the loaf but don't cut all the way through the bottom so that it ends up looking sort of like a Slinky. Brush the butter mixture over all the cut surfaces. Wrap tightly in foil and bake in a 400°F (200°C) oven until your whole kitchen smells insanely good, about 15 minutes.

4   **Spanish-Style Grilled Tomato Toast:** If you have a hot grill going (say, for Fish Kebabs, page 141), slice the loaf of bread and drizzle or brush the slices generously with extra-virgin olive oil. Grill until dark char marks appear on one side. Rub a garlic clove on the grilled side, if you'd like. Cut a tomato in half and rub the cut side into the toast until you're left with only the tomato skin in your hand. Splash with sherry vinegar, sprinkle with flaky salt, and serve hot.

5   **Homemade Croutons:** Cut the bread into 1-inch (2.5 cm) cubes. You can remove the crusts if you prefer—your choice! Place the cubes in a large skillet, drizzle generously with olive oil, and sprinkle with fine sea salt. Cook over medium-low heat, stirring occasionally, until golden brown and crisp on the outside but still tender and chewy inside.

Vegetarian Summer Rolls with Peanut Sauce

Makes 12 rolls

These summer rolls travel well for picnic parties and keep well when hanging around on your table or picnic blanket for a little while. They're also vegetarian and can easily be made vegan by using more vegetable oil in place of the butter. Remember to use tamari (not soy sauce) for any gluten-free guests.

SHIITAKE-CABBAGE FILLING

2 tablespoons vegetable oil

1 tablespoon toasted sesame oil

2 tablespoons unsalted butter

6 ounces (170 g) shiitake mushrooms, stems removed, caps sliced

1 (2-inch/5 cm) piece fresh ginger, peeled and finely grated

3 garlic cloves, finely grated

3 cups (270 g) shredded cabbage

¼ teaspoon fine sea salt

1 tablespoon soy sauce or tamari

2 teaspoons rice vinegar

PEANUT SAUCE

3 garlic cloves, peeled but whole

3 tablespoons rice vinegar

¾ cup (205 g) smooth peanut butter

3 tablespoons soy sauce or tamari

3 tablespoons light or dark brown sugar

2 tablespoons toasted sesame oil

3 to 6 tablespoons ice water

SUMMER ROLLS

12 (9-inch/23 cm) rice paper rounds

1 carrot, peeled and cut into matchsticks

4 ounces (115 g) extra-firm tofu, cut into matchsticks

Handful of fresh Thai basil or regular basil leaves

Handful of fresh mint leaves

Handful of fresh cilantro leaves

Make the shiitake-cabbage filling: In a large skillet, combine the vegetable oil, sesame oil, and butter and warm over medium-high heat. When the butter has melted, add the shiitake mushrooms and stir to coat them in the oil and butter. Cook, without stirring, until golden brown on the undersides, 3 to 4 minutes. Stir and continue cooking until golden brown all over, another 3 to 4 minutes.

Add the ginger, garlic, cabbage, and salt. Cook, stirring often, until the cabbage softens, about 3 minutes. Remove the pan from the heat and mix in the soy sauce and vinegar. Transfer the shiitake-cabbage mixture to a bowl and let cool completely. →

Meanwhile, make the peanut sauce: Using a mortar and pestle or the side of a large knife, crush the garlic to a paste. Transfer the garlic paste to a medium bowl and pour in the vinegar. Let rest for a few minutes so the flavor of the garlic mellows. Whisk in the peanut butter, soy sauce, brown sugar, sesame oil, and 3 tablespoons of ice water. The sauce should be thick but dippable. If you'd like the sauce to be a little looser, whisk in more water, 1 tablespoon at a time. Transfer the peanut sauce to a jar.

Assemble the summer rolls: Rinse out the skillet and fill it with hot water from the tap. Working with one rice paper round at a time, soak it in the hot water until it's pliable, 5 to 20 seconds. Remove the round from the water and lay it flat on a clean work surface.

Keep in mind that you have enough filling for about 12 rolls, and portion it out accordingly. Arrange some shiitake-cabbage, a few matchsticks of the carrot and tofu, and a few herb leaves on the bottom one-third of the round, leaving about 1 inch (2.5 cm) of open rice paper at the bottom edge. Fold in the left and right sides of the rice paper round, then lift the bottom edge up and over the filling. Tightly roll the rice paper to form a compact cylinder. Repeat with the remaining rice paper rounds and fillings.

Slice each roll into thirds and serve the peanut sauce on the side for dipping.

Do Ahead The shiitake-cabbage filling can be made up to 3 days ahead and stored in an airtight container in the fridge. Same with the peanut sauce. Prepping the carrot, tofu, and herbs can take some time, so if you'd like to break up the recipe, you can get those ingredients ready and line them up on a large plate or quarter-sheet pan, cover loosely, and refrigerate until you're ready to roll. Up to 2 hours before serving, you can make the rolls and refrigerate them, covered with a clean, damp kitchen towel so that the wrappers stay nice and pliable.

Crispy Scallion Pancakes and Dipping Sauce Trio

Serves 6

Please every guest in the room by offering not one but three sauces with this savory, umami bomb of a pancake. One is green and bright from fresh cilantro and tart yuzu juice. Another is a mouth-tingling combo of soy and chili crisp. And the third is sweet, dark, and gingery.

SCALLION PANCAKE DOUGH

4 cups (500 g) all-purpose flour, plus more for kneading and rolling

¼ teaspoon fine sea salt

1½ cups (360 g) boiling water

Toasted sesame oil, for brushing

8 scallions, thinly sliced

Vegetable oil, for cooking

CILANTRO-YUZU DIPPING SAUCE

1 bunch fresh cilantro

1 tablespoon toasted sesame oil

Fine sea salt

1 tablespoon yuzu juice

SOY-CHILI DIPPING SAUCE

¼ cup (60 ml) soy sauce or tamari

2 tablespoons rice vinegar

1 tablespoon chili crisp

2 teaspoons white sesame seeds

HOISIN DIPPING SAUCE

½ cup (120 ml) hoisin sauce

1 (2-inch/5 cm) piece fresh ginger, peeled and finely grated

1 garlic clove, minced

2 tablespoons fresh lime juice

Make the scallion pancake dough: In a large bowl, combine the flour and salt. Pour in the boiling water and stir with a wooden spoon until a soft dough forms. Turn out the dough onto a floured work surface and knead it until smooth and elastic, about 5 minutes. Cover and let rest for 30 minutes.

Meanwhile, make the cilantro-yuzu dipping sauce: Rinse the cilantro and, while it's still dripping wet, put it (stems and all) in a food processor or high-powered blender. Add the sesame oil and a pinch of salt and blend to a puree. Pour in the yuzu juice and blend until incorporated. Transfer the cilantro-yuzu sauce to a jar.

Make the soy-chili dipping sauce: In another jar, combine the soy sauce, vinegar, chili crisp, and sesame seeds. Cover the jar and shake briefly to combine. ⟶

Make the hoisin dipping sauce: In a small bowl, whisk together the hoisin, ginger, garlic, and lime juice. Transfer to a third jar.

Divide the dough into 8 equal portions. Using a floured rolling pin, roll each piece into a round about 8 inches (21 cm) in diameter. Brush with a thin layer of sesame oil and scatter about 1 tablespoon of the chopped scallions on top. Roll up the dough into a log, then coil the log around itself (like a snake). Flatten the coil into an 8-inch (21 cm) round about ⅛ inch (3 mm) thick. Repeat to make 8 pancakes.

In a large skillet, heat 1 tablespoon vegetable oil over medium-high heat. Add one pancake to the pan and cook until golden and crisp on the first side, 2 to 3 minutes. Flip and cook on the other side until golden and crisp, another 2 to 3 minutes. Repeat to cook the remaining pancakes.

Cut the pancakes into slices and serve warm, with the dipping sauce trio on the side.

Do Ahead You can make all three dipping sauces up to 3 days ahead. Store them separately, each one in an airtight container like a jar, in the fridge. It's totally fine to make the pancake dough and do the rolling and coiling steps the day before the party. Keep the shaped pancakes in a single layer and covered in the fridge overnight, and make sure to let them warm up to room temperature for several hours before cooking them. Serve them hot and crispy straight out of the pan or keep them hot by placing them on a sheet pan in a 200°F (90°C) oven.

Salmon-Avocado Temaki

Makes 16 small rolls

Temaki are quick and simple to shape and also a nice way for home cooks to serve beautiful sushi, because they're a little easier than nigiri and classic rolls but no less special. You can fill these hand rolls with your favorite sushi-grade fish. Try yellowtail (aka hamachi) or finely chopped fatty tuna (aka toro). Any time you're using raw fish, make sure it is as fresh as can be. Buy it from a local Japanese market or fishmonger and serve it that same day. These hand rolls would pair exceptionally well with Yakitori-Style Tsukune Sauced with Ume Plum Tare (page 167) and/or Furikake Kabocha Moons (page 185).

3 cups (710 ml) water

2 cups (400 g) short-grain white rice, rinsed

1 teaspoon fine sea salt

2 tablespoons rice vinegar

12 ounces (340 g) sashimi-grade skinless salmon fillet

1 tablespoon toasted sesame oil

3 tablespoons soy sauce or tamari

1 large or 2 small avocados

8 sheets nori, cut in half

Furikake, for sprinkling

In a medium saucepan, bring the water to a boil. Add the rice and salt, turn the heat down to medium-low, cover, and cook until all the water has been absorbed, about 18 minutes. Remove from the heat, uncover, and splash in the vinegar. Cover with the lid and let rest for 10 minutes.

Meanwhile, using a very sharp knife, cut the salmon across the grain first into slices and then into cubes that are somewhere between ¼ and ½ inch (6 mm and 1.3 cm). Place them in a shallow dish, pour in the sesame oil and soy sauce, and mix gently. Cut the avocado into thin slices and set them aside.

Dry your hands thoroughly and place a piece of nori, shiny side down, in the palm of your nondominant hand. Spread ¼ to ½ cup (50 to 100 g) of rice in an even layer across the left half of the nori. Sprinkle with some furikake. Arrange a few avocado slices and a heaping spoonful of salmon diagonally across the rice. Cup your palm to bring the bottom-left corner in toward the center of the nori. Tuck it in and roll the nori around the rice into a cone shape. To help the nori stick to itself, put a grain of rice under the end of the nori and gently press to seal. Serve right away.

Tie-Dye Dumplings

Serves 6 to 8

Classic pork and cabbage dumplings get the star treatment here, wrapped in a showstopping, naturally dyed rainbow dough. There are many ways to shape dumplings, some requiring a little skill, but after you practice doing the first few (or watch some YouTube videos), you'll get the hang of it. If your friends love to cook, consider hosting a dumpling-making party as this recipe is especially fun to make as a group project. And each cook gets to eat or take home what they make!

DUMPLING DOUGH

Handful of baby spinach leaves

1⅓ cups minus 1 tablespoon (305 ml) boiling water

1 red beet

5 cups (625 g) all-purpose flour, plus more for rolling

Fine sea salt

1 teaspoon butterfly pea flower powder

FILLING

1½ pounds (680 g) ground pork

4 cups (360 g) shredded napa cabbage

2 bunches fresh chives, chopped

1 (4-inch/10 cm) piece fresh ginger, peeled and finely grated

¼ cup (60 ml) soy sauce

¼ cup (60 ml) toasted sesame oil

FOR SERVING (OPTIONAL)

Soy sauce

Black vinegar

Chili oil

Make the dumpling dough: Place the spinach in a heatproof bowl and pour in ⅓ cup (80 ml) of the boiling water to wilt the leaves. Use an immersion blender to puree until smooth. Strain through a fine-mesh sieve into a liquid measuring cup. There should be ⅓ cup (80 ml) green juice; if there's less, top up with hot water from the tap.

Grate the beet, wrap it in cheesecloth, and squeeze until you get 1 tablespoon beet juice.

Divide the flour evenly among four medium or large bowls—that's 1¼ cups (156 g) of flour per bowl—and add a pinch of salt to each bowl.

To the first bowl, add the butterfly pea flower powder and ⅓ cup (80 ml) boiling water. Stir to incorporate. To the second bowl, add the beet juice and ⅓ cup minus 1 tablespoon (65 ml) boiling water. Stir to incorporate. To the third bowl, pour in the spinach water and stir to incorporate. To the fourth bowl, pour in the remaining ⅓ cup (80 ml) boiling water and stir to incorporate. →

Transfer each of the 4 dough balls to a clean work surface and separately knead each one until smooth, making sure to keep the colors apart, about 5 minutes. If the dough feels stiff, wet your hands with hot tap water and continue kneading. Repeat as necessary. Cover the dough balls and let rest at room temperature for 30 minutes.

Meanwhile, make the filling: In the bowl used for the plain (undyed) dough (it doesn't need to be cleaned), combine the pork, cabbage, chives, ginger, soy sauce, and sesame oil. Mix well.

Fill a small bowl with water and set it nearby.

Divide each dough ball into 2 equal portions and keep them all covered with a clean, damp kitchen towel. Working with one piece at a time, roll each piece of dough into a rope about 16 inches (40 cm) long, dusting with flour as needed. Twist a pink and blue rope around each other and twist a green and white rope around each other. Then twist the 2 twisted ropes around each other to form a very large rope. Repeat with the other dough pieces to make 2 very large ropes. Cut each rope crosswise into 16 equal pieces. Roll out each piece to a flat round about 4 inches (10 cm) in diameter.

Place a dough round in the palm of your nondominant hand. Spoon a rounded ½ tablespoon of filling into the center of the dough round. Dip your finger in the water and use it to moisten the edge of the wrapper. Fold the wrapper in half, around the filling, and pinch the edges closed. Make three pleats on the right side of the curved edge of the dumpling, pinching each pleat firmly to seal, then make three pleats on the left side of the curved edge. The pleats should all point toward the center to give the dumpling a crescent shape. Repeat to form the remaining dumplings.

To cook the dumplings, bring a pot of water to a simmer. Working in batches, add as many dumplings as will fit comfortably in the pot and cook for about 5 minutes.

Arrange the cooked dumplings in a single layer on a serving platter. Serve soy sauce, black vinegar, and chili oil in little bowls on the side.

Do Ahead Make the filling up to 3 days ahead and store it, covered, in the fridge. The dumpling doughs can also be made up to 3 days ahead and stored in an airtight container in the fridge. Let the dough balls warm up to room temperature for 2 hours before rolling. Once the dumplings are shaped, they can be stored in a single layer, loosely covered, in the fridge for 24 hours. Alternatively, they can be frozen until firm and then packaged in ziplock bags and stored in the freezer for up to 3 months. Cook them from frozen for 5 to 7 minutes.

Cherry Tomato and Arugula Pesto Galette

Serves 4 to 6

This galette is as delicious and popular as pizza but will feel just a touch more sophisticated. It has a flaky crust and is topped with cherry tomatoes and a zesty arugula pesto that's made even greener by the addition of pistachios instead of the traditional pine nuts. You can make the dough and pesto ahead of time, so this dish comes together easily on the day of your party.

GALETTE DOUGH

1½ cups (187 g) all-purpose flour, plus more for rolling

1 tablespoon sugar

¾ teaspoon fine sea salt

1½ sticks (6 ounces/170 g) unsalted butter, sliced and chilled

⅓ cup (80 ml) ice-cold water

ARUGULA PESTO

1 cup (20 g) arugula, plus more for topping

¼ cup (5 g) fresh basil leaves

⅓ cup (45 g) pistachios, toasted

1 garlic clove, peeled but whole

Finely grated zest of 1 lemon

1 tablespoon fresh lemon juice

½ teaspoon fine sea salt, plus more to taste

⅓ cup (80 ml) extra-virgin olive oil

FOR ASSEMBLY

3 tablespoons freshly grated Parmigiano-Reggiano cheese

1½ pounds (680 g) cherry tomatoes

Make the galette dough: In a large bowl, stir together the flour, sugar, and salt. Using your fingertips, rub the butter into the flour mixture until the butter pieces are the size of corn kernels. Pour in the water and quickly but gently knead into a ball of dough. Wrap it in plastic and refrigerate for at least 1 hour.

Meanwhile, make the arugula pesto: Using a food processor, combine the arugula, basil, pistachios, garlic, lemon zest, lemon juice, and salt and pulse until finely chopped. Pour in the olive oil all at once and blend until mostly smooth. Taste and season with more salt if needed.

To assemble: When you're ready to bake the galette, preheat the oven to 375°F (190°C). Line a sheet pan with parchment paper.

On a lightly floured surface, roll out the dough into a large round or oval about ⅛ inch (3 mm) thick. Place the dough on the prepared sheet pan. Spread the arugula pesto across the dough, scatter the Parmigiano on

top, and arrange the cherry tomatoes on top of the cheese, leaving bare a 2-inch (5 cm) border around the edges. Fold the dough edges in over the toppings. Chill in the refrigerator (or, even better, the freezer—if it can fit!) for 10 minutes.

Bake the galette for 1 hour, rotating front to back once, until the crust is dark golden brown. Top with arugula and serve hot or warm.

Do Ahead You can make the pesto ahead of time and store it in an airtight container in the refrigerator for up to 3 days. The dough can also be made up to 3 days ahead.

Panelle

Serves 6 to 8

These Aleppo pepper–flecked fritters are crisped to golden-brown perfection, and they're a lovely option to serve to gluten-free friends. Chickpea flour is naturally gluten-free but behaves a bit like wheat flour in that it comes together with water and olive oil into a thick batter. The resulting fritters look like steak fries but have loads of wonderfully earthy flavor.

Olive oil, for greasing the pan

4 cups (950 ml) water

2 cups (185 g) chickpea flour

¼ cup (60 ml) extra-virgin olive oil, plus more for greasing

½ teaspoon fine sea salt

¼ teaspoon Aleppo chile powder, plus more (optional) for sprinkling

Vegetable oil, for frying

Flaky sea salt

Grease a sheet pan with olive oil.

In a large saucepan, bring the water to a boil. Slowly stream in the chickpea flour while whisking constantly to prevent lumps. Continue whisking until the mixture bubbles at a gentle simmer. Add the olive oil, fine salt, and Aleppo pepper. Cook, whisking, for 1 minute. Transfer the chickpea batter to the prepared sheet pan, spreading it out to an even thickness. Let cool to room temperature, then refrigerate until completely chilled, at least 1 hour and up to 3 days.

Line a sheet pan with a wire rack or clean brown paper bags. Pour about ½ inch (1.3 cm) vegetable oil into a large skillet and heat over medium-high heat for 2 minutes.

Meanwhile, cut the set chickpea mixture into fries about the size of your middle finger.

Working in batches, add some fries to the hot oil, leaving about ½ inch (1.3 cm) of space around each fry, and cook, stirring and flipping, until golden brown and crisp on all sides, 3 to 5 minutes. Transfer the fritters to the rack or paper bags. Sprinkle the fritters with flaky salt and more Aleppo pepper, if you'd like, and serve hot.

Smoky Shrimp Tostadas

Serves 6

The mix of roasted onions and sweet bell peppers plus avocado and queso fresco makes these smoky shrimp tostadas special—and beautifully colored. This dish pulls its weight and works nicely as a filling side, but it can also be served as one of a couple of main dishes. For a vegan version, swap the shrimp for cooked pinto or black beans. If you can't find store-bought tostadas, brush vegetable oil on both sides of corn tortillas and crisp them in a hot skillet on the stovetop.

2 red bell peppers, sliced

2 yellow bell peppers, sliced

1 large white onion, cut into 1-inch (2.5 cm) wedges

8 tablespoons (120 ml) grapeseed oil

1 teaspoon ground cumin

Fine sea salt

2 canned chipotle peppers in adobo sauce, plus 1 tablespoon adobo sauce (from one 7-ounce/200 g can)

1¼ pounds (570 g) medium or large shrimp, peeled and deveined

2 teaspoons cornstarch

6 corn tostadas

FOR SERVING

Sliced avocado

Queso fresco, crumbled

Fresh cilantro leaves (optional)

Preheat the oven to 425°F (220°C).

On a sheet pan, toss together the bell peppers, onion, 5 tablespoons (75 ml) of the grapeseed oil, cumin, and ¾ teaspoon salt and spread the vegetables out on the pan. Roast, stirring once or twice, until tender and browned in a few places, about 30 minutes.

Meanwhile, use a blender to puree the chipotle peppers with the adobo sauce.

Place the shrimp in a large bowl and sprinkle with the cornstarch and ½ teaspoon salt. Pour in the chipotle puree and mix well.

In a large skillet, warm the remaining 3 tablespoons grapeseed oil over medium-high heat. Add the chipotle shrimp and cook, using tongs to flip the shrimp once, until just barely cooked through, 2 to 3 minutes.

To serve, divide the shrimp among the tostadas and top with the roasted peppers and onion, avocado, queso fresco, and cilantro (if using).

Ejjeh-Inspired Frittata and Labne Sauce

Serves 8 to 10

The Lebanese egg pancakes called ejjeh are typically the size of drink coasters or smaller, and they are a quick meal eaten for breakfast, lunch, dinner, or really any time of day. In this variation on the dish, the traditional ejjeh ingredients of fresh herbs and zucchini combine to make one large frittata. There's something wonderfully communal about serving a whole frittata at a party, like a birthday cake that everyone gets a slice of.

2 small or 1 large zucchini

Fine sea salt

4 scallions, finely chopped

1 cup (20 g) fresh flat-leaf parsley leaves, finely chopped

1 cup (20 g) fresh dill, finely chopped

1 cup (20 g) fresh mint leaves, finely chopped

8 large eggs

1 teaspoon baking powder

1½ cups (430 g) labne or Greek yogurt

2 tablespoons extra-virgin olive oil

Finely grated zest and juice of 1 lemon

1 tablespoon za'atar

Preheat the oven to 300°F (150°C).

Grate the zucchini on the large holes of a box grater into a fine-mesh sieve set over a bowl. Sprinkle with salt and let rest for about 10 minutes.

Use your hands to squeeze as much liquid as possible from the zucchini, then place the drained zucchini in a large bowl. (There should be about 2 cups.) Mix in the scallions, parsley, dill, mint, eggs, baking powder, 2 teaspoons salt, and ½ cup (145 g) of the labne. Beat with a fork until just combined.

In a 12-inch (30 cm) ovenproof skillet, heat the olive oil over medium-high heat and swirl to coat the pan. Pour in the herby-egg mixture and use a wooden spoon to stir for 1½ minutes. Transfer the skillet to the oven and cook until just barely set in the center when poked with the tip of a knife, about 20 minutes.

Meanwhile, in a small serving bowl, stir together the lemon zest, lemon juice, za'atar, ¼ teaspoon salt, and the remaining 1 cup labne.

Let the frittata cool in the skillet for about 10 minutes, then turn it out onto a serving plate. Cut into wedges and serve with the labne sauce.

Garlic Knot Waffles

Makes 6 to 8 waffles (depending on size)

People love waffles. You love them, I love them, and your guests will love these savory ones that taste like cheesy garlic knots but with a crisp waffle exterior. They are the perfect unexpected side to Bavette with Chimichurri (page 153) or any hearty main that needs a starchy sidekick.

6 garlic cloves, minced

4 tablespoons (½ stick/55 g) unsalted butter, plus more for the waffle iron

2 tablespoons extra-virgin olive oil

2 cups (250 g) all-purpose flour

¼ cup (25 g) freshly grated Parmigiano-Reggiano cheese, plus more for serving

1 teaspoon baking powder

½ teaspoon baking soda

½ teaspoon fine sea salt

4 large eggs

1 cup (240 ml) whole milk

1 cup (250 g) plain whole-milk yogurt

¼ cup (5 g) fresh flat-leaf parsley leaves, finely chopped

In a small saucepan, cook the garlic in the butter and oil over low heat until very fragrant and light golden, about 5 minutes. Remove from the heat and let cool slightly.

In a large bowl, combine the flour, Parmigiano, baking powder, baking soda, and salt.

In another bowl, vigorously whisk the eggs until foamy, then whisk in the milk, yogurt, parsley, and cooled garlic butter. Pour this wet mixture into the bowl of flour and whisk until no lumps remain.

Preheat the oven to 200°F (90°C) and place a sheet pan in the oven. Heat a waffle iron.

Butter the inside surfaces of the waffle iron. Spoon ¼ to ½ cup (60 to 120 ml) of the batter onto the waffle iron, close the lid, and cook until crisp and golden brown, following the manufacturer's instructions. Transfer the cooked waffle to the sheet pan inside the oven to keep warm while you cook the remaining batter.

Cut the waffles into quarters and serve hot, sprinkled with Parmigiano.

Do Ahead The best way to make these ahead of time is to undercook the waffles a tiny bit (about a minute or two less) and then let them cool to room temperature before freezing them in a ziplock bag. To reheat, simply pop them into a toaster.

Toothpick Gnocchi with Oregano Bread Crumbs

Serves 4

You may be used to eating gnocchi as a main at your favorite Italian restaurant, but these little potato dumplings make excellent finger food when pierced with a handy toothpick. Tossed with pesto and showered with oregano bread crumbs and Parmigiano, they're the perfect bite between sips of a cold drink like sparkling wine or a spritzy mocktail (how about the Nonalcoholic Chinotto Spritz, page 248?). This recipe uses store-bought gnocchi for a stress-free side.

6 tablespoons (85 g) unsalted butter

½ cup (30 g) panko bread crumbs

2 garlic cloves, minced

1 tablespoon dried oregano

¼ teaspoon red pepper flakes

Fine sea salt

1 (18-ounce/510 g) package shelf-stable potato gnocchi

1 tablespoon extra-virgin olive oil

Freshly ground black pepper

½ cup (125 g) store-bought pesto

¼ cup (25 g) freshly grated Parmigiano-Reggiano cheese

In a small saucepan, cook the butter over medium heat until it turns a deep grizzly-bear brown and smells nutty, 4 to 5 minutes.

Pour half of the browned butter into a large skillet over medium heat. Add the bread crumbs, garlic, oregano, pepper flakes, and ¼ teaspoon salt and cook, stirring occasionally, until the bread crumbs are toasted and crunchy, 3 to 5 minutes. Transfer to a bowl and set aside.

Place the same skillet over medium-high heat. Add the remaining browned butter, followed by the gnocchi, breaking up any gnocchi that are stuck together. Cover the pan and cook the gnocchi, without stirring, until they turn golden brown on their undersides and release from the pan, 2 to 4 minutes. Drizzle in the olive oil, sprinkle with salt and pepper to taste, and cook until golden on the other side, about 2 minutes more. Stir in the pesto.

Remove the pan from the heat and sprinkle the gnocchi with the Parmigiano and oregano bread crumbs. Toss to coat the gnocchi, then slide them all onto a platter. Stick toothpicks into the gnocchi and serve steaming hot.

Saffron Couscous with Cauliflower, Chickpeas, and Pomegranate

Serves 6 to 8

A gorgeous, satisfying, and vibrant side dish to serve alongside roasted meat or vegetables. You can easily vegan-ify this couscous by using vegetable stock. The tiniest pinch of saffron brings lots of color and an appealing slightly floral aroma to this dish.

1 head cauliflower, cut into ¾-inch (2 cm) florets

¼ cup (60 ml) plus 2 tablespoons olive oil

1 teaspoon ground turmeric

Fine sea salt and freshly ground black pepper

1 (15.5-ounce/439 g) can chickpeas, drained and rinsed

3 cups (710 ml) good-quality chicken broth, vegetable stock, or water

2 cups (345 g) couscous

Pinch of saffron threads

3 big handfuls of baby spinach

1 cup (175 g) pomegranate seeds

½ cup (10 g) fresh flat-leaf parsley, finely chopped

1 lemon, halved

Preheat the oven to 400°F (200°C).

Place the cauliflower florets on a sheet pan, drizzle with ¼ cup (60 ml) of the olive oil, and season with the turmeric, 1 teaspoon salt, and lots of pepper. Use your hands to toss until evenly coated, then spread the florets out on the pan. Roast, stirring once, for 15 minutes. Add the chickpeas and continue roasting until the chickpeas are golden brown and the cauliflower is browned in some places and tender, 10 to 15 minutes more.

Meanwhile, in a medium saucepan, bring the chicken broth to a boil. Add the remaining 2 tablespoons olive oil, the couscous, the saffron, and 1 teaspoon salt. Stir well. Remove from the heat, cover with a lid, and let rest until the couscous has absorbed all the liquid, about 10 minutes.

Transfer the couscous to a large serving bowl or platter with a lip. Add the spinach and then the cauliflower-chickpea mixture. Mix gently, just enough to incorporate the spinach and let it wilt a little from the residual heat. Scatter the pomegranate seeds and parsley on top, squeeze lemon juice over everything, and serve.

Extraordinary Green Leafy Salad

Serves 6

A green salad goes with every meal. What makes this green salad extraordinary? First, it's made from three different kinds of lettuce plus fresh parsley leaves and dill. Also, every effort is taken to ensure the greens are squeaky clean and thoroughly dried. (Nothing ruins a salad faster than soggy greens.) The dressing hits all the right notes: sweet (honey), tart (lemon juice and vinegar), and subtly savory (just a dab of Dijon mustard). And last but definitely not least, the salad is served tall and proud, piled up high and reaching for the heavens.

2 heads butter lettuce

2 romaine hearts

4 cups (80 g) arugula

1 cup (20 g) fresh flat-leaf parsley leaves

¼ cup (5 g) fresh dill

DRESSING

1 small shallot, very finely chopped

1 garlic clove, crushed to a paste

¼ cup (60 ml) fresh lemon juice

1 tablespoon red wine vinegar or sherry vinegar

1 teaspoon honey

Fine sea salt

Dijon mustard

6 tablespoons (90 ml) extra-virgin olive oil

1 tablespoon warm water

Freshly ground black pepper

Trim the bottoms off the butter lettuces and discard any bruised outer leaves. Separate the heads into individual leaves. Do the same with the romaine hearts. Rinse the butter lettuce, romaine, arugula, parsley, and dill by swishing them in a large bowl of cold water. Dry the lettuces and herbs thoroughly in a salad spinner. Line a very large bowl with a clean kitchen towel and place the clean lettuces and herbs in the bowl. Refrigerate, uncovered, while you make the dressing.

Make the dressing: Place the chopped shallot in a small fine-mesh sieve and rinse under cold water for 30 seconds, then transfer the shallot to a small bowl. Add the garlic, lemon juice, vinegar, honey, and a pinch of salt. Let rest for 5 minutes.

Dip the tines of a clean fork into the mustard jar. When you lift the fork, a small amount of mustard will cling to the tines. Dunk the fork into the lemon juice mixture and stir to incorporate. Pour in the olive oil and water and stir until emulsified. ⟶

Remove the kitchen towel from the bowl of clean lettuce and herbs. Season the greens with ½ teaspoon salt and lots of pepper. Drizzle in about half of the dressing and use your hands to gently toss the salad. Taste a leaf and add more dressing if you like. Pile the salad high in a bowl or on a platter and serve right away, with any extra dressing in a small bowl on the side for guests to add if they want.

Do Ahead You can clean all your lettuces and herbs and store them in the refrigerator as the recipe directs up to 1 day in advance of serving. The salad dressing can be made up to 1 week ahead and stored in an airtight container in the refrigerator.

SECRETS TO THE BEST SALADS

- **When in doubt, keep it simple.** High-quality greens don't need much to be delicious. Seek out in-season leaves at farmers' markets or find a friend who grows their own lettuce. (Maybe that friend is you?)

- **Rinse! Your! Produce!** You really will taste the difference when every speck of dirt has been rinsed away and there are only pristine greens on the plate. They practically sparkle.

- **Balance flavors.** When you're making a loaded salad, a rich ingredient like chopped salami benefits from the presence of something tart like pickled peppers.

- **Don't forget about the importance of crunch.** Croutons are a go-to, of course, but you could also try adding chopped toasted nuts or roasted pumpkin seeds (aka pepitas).

- **Skip the leafy greens altogether.** Avocado and citrus fruit make a beautiful salad when drizzled with olive oil and sprinkled with salt.

Green Bean, Watermelon Radish, and Crunchy Quinoa Salad

Serves 6

This salad doesn't have any leafy greens. It's hearty from green beans and a generous shower of crunchy quinoa. It can hold its own as a satisfying dish in a vegan menu, and it also pairs well with meaty mains like Bavette with Chimichurri (page 153).

½ cup (85 g) quinoa (any color), rinsed well

1 cup (240 ml) water

Fine sea salt

1 small garlic clove, peeled

3 tablespoons fresh lemon juice

1½ teaspoons good-quality red wine vinegar

Freshly ground black pepper

Dijon mustard

½ cup (120 ml) extra-virgin olive oil

1 pound (450 g) haricots verts, stem ends trimmed (you can leave their little tails on)

8 ounces (225 g) watermelon radishes, scrubbed

Flaky sea salt

In a small saucepan, combine the rinsed quinoa, water, and a pinch of fine salt. Bring to a boil, then adjust the heat so that the water simmers gently. Cook, uncovered, until the quinoa has absorbed all the water, 12 to 15 minutes. Remove the pan from the heat, cover, and let steam for 5 minutes. Fluff the quinoa with a fork and transfer it to a plate lined with a clean kitchen towel or paper towels to absorb any extra moisture.

Meanwhile, using a mortar and pestle or the side of a large knife, crush the garlic and a pinch of fine salt to a smooth paste. Transfer to a small bowl and stir in the lemon juice, vinegar, ¼ teaspoon fine salt, and lots of black pepper. Dip the tines of a clean fork into the mustard jar. When you lift the fork, a small amount of mustard will cling to the tines. Dunk the fork into the lemon juice mixture and stir to incorporate. Pour in ¼ cup (60 ml) of the olive oil and stir until the dressing is emulsified.

In a large skillet, warm the remaining ¼ cup (60 ml) olive oil over medium heat and add the cooked quinoa. Cook, stirring occasionally, until the quinoa is golden brown and crunchy, 5 to 10 minutes. Transfer to a plate and let cool. ⟶

Wipe out the skillet and fill it with hot water. Season the water generously with fine salt and bring to a boil. Add the haricots verts and cook until bright green and tender but still a little crunchy, 1½ minutes. Drain and transfer to a large serving platter.

Using a mandoline or a sharp knife, slice the radishes as thinly as possible. Add them to the platter with the green beans. Drizzle the dressing over the radishes and beans and use your hands to gently toss. Sprinkle the crunchy quinoa over the top, finish with a few pinches of flaky salt, and serve.

Do Ahead The dressing can be made up to 1 week ahead and stored in an airtight container in the fridge. You can cook the quinoa up to 3 days ahead and store, covered, in the fridge. But wait to fry the quinoa in the olive oil until the day of the party.

Radish and Avocado Salad

Serves 6

The crunch of radish and the creaminess of ripe avocado combine for a beautifully balanced salad that would be equally at home in a meal with either Mexican or Mediterranean flavors. Best to slice the radish paper-thin—use a mandoline if you have one or a razor-sharp knife if you don't.

2 avocados

2 scallions, thinly sliced, white and green parts kept separate

1 bunch fresh cilantro, bottom stems trimmed

Finely grated zest and juice of 3 limes

Fine sea salt

6 tablespoons (90 ml) extra-virgin olive oil

1 bunch radishes or 1 softball-size watermelon radish

3 Little Gems or 1 large romaine heart, roughly torn or chopped

¼ small head red cabbage, sliced into thin ribbons

Freshly ground black pepper

In a food processor, combine one-quarter of one of the avocados, the scallion whites, half of the cilantro, the lime zest and juice, and ½ teaspoon salt. Blend until finely chopped. With the machine running, drizzle in the olive oil and continue blending until fully combined. Set the dressing aside.

Slice the radishes as thinly as possible. If using watermelon radish, peel it first and cut it into quarters before slicing. Place the radish slices in a very large serving bowl and add the romaine, cabbage, scallion greens, and the remaining cilantro. Season with a pinch or two of salt and lots of pepper.

Just before serving, cut the remaining avocado into bite-size pieces or thin slices and add them to the bowl. Add the dressing and toss gently.

Cara Cara, Hazelnut, and Ruby Chicories Salad

Serves 6 to 8

This cheerful and bright salad will enliven any winter meal. Seek out Cara Cara oranges for their sweet flavor and rosy color. If you can't find them, you could sub pink grapefruit or another citrus fruit.

1½ cups (215 g) raw (skin-on) hazelnuts

2 large or 4 small red Belgian endives

2 small or 1 large head radicchio

1 garlic clove, pounded to a paste

3 tablespoons fresh lemon juice

1 tablespoon sherry vinegar

Fine sea salt

2 teaspoons honey

5 tablespoons (75 ml) extra-virgin olive oil

2 Cara Cara oranges

Freshly ground black pepper

Preheat the oven to 350°F (180°C).

Spread the hazelnuts on a sheet pan and toast in the oven until golden brown, 10 to 12 minutes.

Meanwhile, trim off the base of the endives and gently separate them into individual leaves, trimming a bit more off the base as needed to detach the inner leaves. Separate the radicchio into individual leaves and tear them into smaller pieces. Place the endive and radicchio in a very large bowl.

In a small bowl, combine the garlic, lemon juice, vinegar, and ¼ teaspoon salt. Let rest for 5 minutes to allow the garlic flavor to mellow. Use a fork or small whisk to stir in the honey and olive oil.

Using a sharp knife, suprême both oranges: Cut off the top and bottom of an orange and stand the fruit on your cutting board on a cut side so it doesn't roll around. Place the blade of your knife at the top of the orange and cut down, tracing the curved line of the fruit, to remove the peel, white pith, and membranes to expose the fruit. Rotate the orange and continue cutting away the peel and pith until you've removed it all. Go back and trim any pith still clinging to the fruit. Holding the orange in your nondominant hand, cut along each thin white membrane to release the segments of fruit. Repeat with the other orange. ⟶

Season the endive and radicchio with a few big pinches of salt and lots of pepper. Drizzle most of the dressing over the salad. Toss gently with your hands until the leaves are evenly coated. Taste and add more dressing, if you like. Transfer the salad to a large serving platter. Top with the orange segments, letting most of them rest on top of the leaves and allowing some to fall through to lower layers. Coarsely chop the toasted hazelnuts and scatter them over the top. Serve.

Do Ahead Toast the hazelnuts up to 1 week ahead and store in an airtight container at room temperature. The dressing can be made up to 1 week ahead and stored in an airtight container in the fridge. Before serving, dip a leaf in the dressing to taste, and if you think it seems a tiny bit flat and in need of some perking up, stir in a squeeze of fresh lemon juice. You can suprême the oranges up to 3 days ahead and store them in the fridge.

Rose-Chile King Trumpet Mushrooms and Sautéed Greens

Serves 6 to 8

This combo of rose petals and guajillo chiles is inspired by the Mediterranean condiment rose harissa, which is a spicy paste made from pureed fresh chile peppers, spices (typically cumin and coriander seeds), and rose petals or rose water. The rose petals in this dish impart a subtly floral flavor, but don't worry, they won't overwhelm the earthy mushrooms and sautéed greens. Make sure you use dried rose petals intended for culinary purposes (which should be from flowers that haven't been sprayed with pesticides). Both the mushrooms and the greens in this recipe are flexible and can be substituted based on what's available, but you'll want to look for a chunky mushroom like king trumpet and greens that are dark as shaded forest like lacinato kale.

2 ounces (55 g) dried guajillo chiles

¼ cup (10 g) dried rose petals

½ cup (120 ml) boiling water

7 garlic cloves, 3 pounded to a paste and 4 sliced

6 tablespoons (90 ml) plus ¼ cup (60 ml) extra-virgin olive oil

Fine sea salt

3 pounds (1.4 kg) king trumpet mushrooms

½ cup (120 ml) white wine or water

1 large bunch lacinato kale, stemmed and midribs removed

½ lemon

Preheat the oven to 425°F (220°C).

Break the dried chiles into small pieces, keeping the seeds and discarding the stems, and place in a spice grinder or high-powered blender. Pulse until ground to a coarse powder. Add the rose petals and pulse a few times to incorporate them. Transfer the rose-chile mixture to a small bowl. Stir in a splash of the boiling water to rehydrate the roses and chiles. Let them absorb it, then stir in a little more boiling water, incrementally adding as much water as they'll take. Mix in the garlic paste, 6 tablespoons (90 ml) of the olive oil, and ¾ teaspoon salt.

Use a clean, damp towel to wipe away any dirt from the mushrooms. Pat them thoroughly dry.

Place the mushrooms in a large bowl, add the rose-chile sauce, and toss gently until evenly coated. Transfer the mushrooms to a sheet pan

and spread them out in a single layer. Roast, flipping once, until nicely browned and tender, about 25 minutes.

Meanwhile, in a large stainless-steel skillet, warm the remaining ¼ cup (60 ml) olive oil over medium heat. Add the sliced garlic and cook, stirring often, until golden, about 2 minutes. Increase the heat to medium-high, pour in the wine, and add the kale. Cook, stirring occasionally, until the liquid evaporates and the kale wilts to tenderness, about 5 minutes. Season with a few pinches of salt.

Transfer the sautéed greens to a large platter and top with the roasted mushrooms. Squeeze some lemon juice over everything and serve.

Salt-and-Vinegar Cauliflower and Brussels

Serves 6 to 8

If you like the sour and umami flavors of salt-and-vinegar chips, you'll love this side dish of roasted brassicas seasoned with sweet sherry vinegar and flaky salt. Crumbles of fresh Spanish-style chorizo add some smoky depth of flavor and heft. For a vegan variation, use soy-rizo.

1 large head cauliflower

1½ pounds (680 g) Brussels sprouts

½ cup (120 ml) plus 2 tablespoons extra-virgin olive oil

Fine sea salt

¾ teaspoon smoked paprika

Freshly ground black pepper

8 ounces (225 g) fresh Mexican-style chorizo or soy-rizo

3 tablespoons sherry vinegar

¼ cup (5 g) fresh flat-leaf parsley, finely chopped

Finely grated zest of 1 lemon

Flaky sea salt

Preheat the oven to 500°F (260°C).

Cut the cauliflower into bite-size florets. Trim the Brussels sprouts and cut them into slices ¼ inch (6 mm) thick. Place the cauliflower and Brussels sprouts in a large bowl. Toss with ½ cup (120 ml) of the olive oil, 1 teaspoon fine salt, the smoked paprika, and lots of black pepper.

Heat a large ovenproof skillet over medium-high heat for 1 minute. Add the remaining 2 tablespoons olive oil and the chorizo and cook, stirring occasionally with a wooden spoon, until broken up into crumbly bits and well browned, 3 to 4 minutes. Use a slotted spoon to transfer the cooked chorizo to a small bowl.

Increase the heat under the skillet to high. Heat a second large ovenproof skillet over high heat. Divide the cauliflower and Brussels sprouts between the two skillets. Cook, stirring only once or twice, until golden brown in a few places. Transfer the skillets to the oven and roast the vegetables until browned in a few more places, about 5 minutes. Stir and continue roasting until the vegetables are tender, 3 to 5 minutes more.

Transfer the roasted vegetables to a serving platter. Drizzle with the vinegar, scatter on the cooked chorizo, and toss gently. Sprinkle with the parsley, lemon zest, and a couple of pinches of flaky salt and serve.

Do Ahead You can make this recipe all the way through tossing the roasted vegetables with the vinegar and chorizo (or soy-rizo). Let cool to room temperature and store, covered, in the fridge for up to 3 days. Reheat gently in a 200°F (90°C) oven, stirring once or twice, until hot all the way through, about 10 minutes. Just before serving, sprinkle with the parsley, lemon zest, and flaky salt.

Blistered Padrón Peppers on Avocado Crema

Serves 6 to 8

Avocado crema is like a perfectly smooth and extra-creamy guacamole. It's terrific as a dip, dolloped on a taco, or, as it is here, spread across a platter and topped with blistered Padrón peppers. Most Padrón peppers are mild, but occasionally you'll come across a spicy one. If you can't find them in markets, use the strikingly similar shishitos or another not-so-fiery pepper like sweet Italian frying peppers.

1 garlic clove, finely chopped

2 tablespoons fresh lime juice

1 avocado, halved and pitted

¼ cup (55 g) Mexican crema or
  sour cream

¼ teaspoon fine sea salt

2 tablespoons grapeseed oil

1 pound (450 g) Padrón peppers

Flaky sea salt

In a blender, combine the garlic and lime juice. Let rest to mellow the garlic's sharp edge for about 5 minutes. Scoop in the avocado and add the crema and fine salt. Blend until completely smooth.

Heat a large cast-iron skillet over medium-high heat for 1 minute. Add 1 tablespoon of the grapeseed oil and half the peppers to the hot skillet, stir to coat the peppers in the oil, and cook, without stirring, until the peppers are dark brown in some places, about 3 minutes. Give them a good stir and then continue cooking, without stirring, until tender, 2 to 3 minutes more. Transfer the blistered peppers to a plate and sprinkle with flaky salt. Repeat with the remaining 1 tablespoon grapeseed oil and peppers. (Alternatively, cook the peppers in two skillets at the same time.)

Spread the avocado crema across a platter. Top with the blistered peppers and serve.

The Art of Serving

You've figured out your menu, gone grocery shopping, and cooked delicious food for the party (check, check, check!), but there's still a crucial part of hosting that's left to do—the art of serving. How you share the food and drinks makes a big difference. Think about it like gift-giving. A wonderful gift can be made even more special when it's gorgeously wrapped in paper, adorned with a ribbon, accompanied by a thoughtfully written card, and, perhaps most important, presented with love. All the same things are true when we serve food at parties. Here's how to do it in style.

LET THE DRINKS FLOW

First things first: Let's have a drink. Getting a glass in each guest's hand as soon as you can is the best advice for hosting magic. Make things easy by offering wine, or if you want to serve cocktails, simplify by making a batch cocktail like Negroni Pitcher (page 264). And if you want to give options, have both on hand. Be sure to always offer something nonalcoholic that's a step above plain water. Doing so takes any pressure off a guest who isn't drinking alcohol. How about Nonalcoholic Sparkling Strawberry-Rhubarb Elixir (page 250), Mock Tiki Punch (page 263), or fizzy Nonalcoholic Raspberry-Lime Spritz (page 249)?

HOW TO POUR BEER AND WINE

If you're serving someone a beer, open it and offer a chilled glass. One great thing about a beer is that you can really drink it out of any glass you like (or, of course, straight from the bottle or can!), but a chilled glass is much better than a room-temperature one. A frosty glass feels like such a special hosting touch; just remember to put the glasses in your freezer at least an hour or two before you plan to use them.

For wine, you might think that filling a glass nearly to the brim is a generous gesture, but there's something about a too-full glass of wine that's unappetizing—not to mention unwieldy. The standard pour in restaurants is five ounces, which amounts to five glasses in each bottle of wine. However, when you're drinking wine at home, a better strategy is to consider the glass itself. For classic stemmed wine glasses, or another glass of a similar shape, stop pouring when the wine reaches the widest part of the bowl. Filling to this point allows for someone to swirl the wine without spilling. (But is swirling for snobs? Nope, it simply aerates the wine and helps to enhance the aromas and flavors, so swirl away if it makes you happy.) When in doubt or when using a nontraditional wine glass, aim for somewhere around or a little above halfway full. There's one notable exception: a champagne flute. The tall, slender shape of a flute is meant to show off champagne's rising tiny bubbles, so keep pouring until you've filled the flute about two-thirds full. Remember, you can always top off guests' glasses, but once you've overpoured, there's no going back.

HOW MUCH FOOD IS ENOUGH FOOD?

Of all the worries you might have about hosting a party, the greatest one usually relates to whether there will be enough food. Of course, you want your friends and family to leave the party feeling full and satisfied. In general, your best bet is to overestimate a little bit. There's no real rule of thumb, but broadly, for every person, consider making enough food to fill 1½ plates (the ½ plate is for when they go back to get seconds). The ideal scenario is a table with dishes that have another few servings if anyone is still hungry. That food becomes leftovers and you've got your meals planned for the next day or two.

Win-win! But estimating how much guests will eat is easier said than done. Appetites vary widely. Also, that yield line in a recipe can be subjective depending on what a serving size means to you or your fellow eaters. A dish that serves six of my friends might be enough for eight of yours. Adding drinks to the meal can also affect your guests' appetites. The point is: It's impossible to know exactly how much food you'll need. So, what's a host to do? A fantastic strategy is to build some flexibility into the menu. Offer several different kinds of dishes and use filling foods like bread to your advantage. Buy an extra loaf of bread from the bakery and don't put it on the dining table until the first loaf has been eaten. If there's something that will keep in your pantry (like crackers) or some food you know you'll be happy to eat later, consider stocking up with some backups.

BUFFET VS. FAMILY-STYLE VS. RESTAURANT-STYLE

Broadly, there are two different ways you can serve food to guests at a party. The first option is a buffet—setting out all the dishes for everyone to serve themselves. A buffet in the kitchen feels homey and warm and is ideal for meals when you're serving foods with a lot of toppings to choose from or when you want guests to have flexibility in how their food is assembled, like for Taco Night (page 287) or a mezze spread. Another bonus of a buffet is that the food can be kept on the stove over low heat to stay warm. Set your table with plates and silverware beforehand and invite guests to grab their own plate and serve themselves. Or you can simply stack the plates and use them to mark the start of the buffet line. Buffet serving is a great option for large parties, where passing food around a table would become a rather slow and awkward process. And a buffet can also be nice when you are hosting a mixed crowd where guests might feel shy calling across the table for something they want.

Option number two for serving food is when guests sit down together at a table and pass platters around until everyone has what they'd like. Allowing each guest to pass the dishes around will create a more intimate dining experience than a buffet, and it usually has the sweet outcome of bonding people together. Despite the name "family-style," this way of serving food isn't necessarily more casual than a buffet. You can make family-style feel formal by serving fancy main dishes like Bavette with Chimichurri (page 153) or Slow-Roasted Steelhead Trout with Shiso Salad (page 147) and by bringing something celebratory like Pistachio Butter Cake with Apricot and Candied Rose Petals (page 197) to the table for everyone to pause and join in singing "Happy Birthday" or raising a glass to the guest of honor.

And, of course, there is a third serving option, which you might call "restaurant-style," where you plate each guest's food in the kitchen and then bring it out to them. I love eating in restaurants, but your home is not meant to be a restaurant, and there's something special about hosting a party and serving food in ways that your guests can't get elsewhere. So, to create that unique party feeling, your best bet is opting for either buffet or family-style. To figure out which way is better for your party, consider both the menu (would your dishes be well suited to a buffet?) and the guest list (does everyone know one another?).

COOKING AHEAD

Cooking ahead is a crucial part of creating a successful party. Nobody wants to be running around and stressed out while guests are asking "What can I do to help?" with wide-eyed looks of concern. The host's energy will be matched by the guests. If you are relaxed and under control, then your guests will also enjoy the party. Even so, the reality is that some foods and drinks just taste better when they're made (or finished) immediately before serving. That means that when you are planning your menu, try to have only a couple of dishes that require your full attention at the last minute before they're served. If your main is best served immediately, choose starters and sides that can be prepared earlier

in the day. Always make sure your menu has at least something that can be made the day before and simply reheated to serve. You'll feel relieved and under control knowing that one part is done.

Leafy salads are best dressed at the last minute, although you can prep all the ingredients and the dressing ahead of time. Shaken cocktails are at their prime during the moments after they are poured into glasses, so put a friend or two on bartender duty, or choose a make-ahead drink like Mai Tai

Punch (page 260). Always read your recipes far ahead of the party and make sense of what steps can be done ahead. Do everything that you can in advance and save only the finishing touches for when your guests have arrived. Do be sure to safely store any food you've cooked ahead of time, whether that's in the refrigerator or tightly wrapped at room temperature. Perishable foods should be kept cold and then thoroughly heated before serving. When you're reheating foods, go slowly and use low heat.

Mains

When we are planning a menu, a lot of us often overstress about the main dish, worrying that it's going to make or break the party. But a menu doesn't hinge on its main. Instead, the main should just be a substantial dish that offers some oomph and leaves everyone feeling full and satisfied. Mains don't always need to be meaty, although they can be if you'd like. A whole brisket (page 156) looks mightily impressive in the center of a table, but you can capture that same energy by serving a mounded platter of Vegetarian Nachos with Sweet Potato, Pintos en Adobo, and Cotija (page 178). And who wouldn't thrill at the sight of Butternut Raviolini with Fried Sage Butter Sauce (page 188)? Hand-shaped pasta feels so special and worthy of being the centerpiece of a meal. Just try to ignore any so-called rules about what you're "supposed" to serve as a main course; instead, cook the dishes that you and your guests love, and keep in mind the spirit of abundance.

Fish Kebabs

Serves 6 to 8

Shish kebabs become fish kebabs in this satisfying pescatarian main course seasoned with a finely calibrated mix of chile powder, cumin, and cinnamon. It's perfect for grilling season and casual outdoor hangs at any time of day. The fish marinates in a bath of tangy lime juice, which will start to cook the fish and turn it into ceviche if you let it go too long. So, for this recipe, don't worry about planning too far ahead of time; fish kebabs are ready for all your spontaneous parties. If you're not a cilantro person, try flat-leaf parsley here instead.

2 pounds (910 g) firm fish steaks or thick fillets, such as swordfish, halibut, or mahi-mahi

⅓ cup (80 ml) extra-virgin olive oil, plus more for brushing

⅓ cup (80 ml) fresh lime juice

8 garlic cloves, pounded to a paste

¼ cup (5 g) cilantro, finely chopped, plus more for serving

1½ teaspoons Aleppo chile powder or other ground chiles

1 teaspoon ground cumin

Pinch of ground cinnamon

2 teaspoons fine sea salt, plus more as needed

1 pint (12 ounces/340 g) cherry tomatoes

1 lime, cut into wedges

If using wooden skewers, soak them in water for at least 30 minutes.

Cut the fish into 1-inch (2.5 cm) cubes and place them in a large bowl. You don't have to break out a ruler for this, but do try to make the pieces approximately the same size so that they cook in the same amount of time. Add the olive oil, lime juice, garlic, cilantro, chile powder, cumin, cinnamon, and salt. Mix well. Let marinate at room temperature for 20 to 30 minutes. Don't go longer than that as the lime juice will start to cook the fish and turn it into ceviche!

Prepare a charcoal grill (or heat a grill pan over medium-high heat). Brush the grates (or pan) with oil to prevent sticking.

Thread the marinated fish cubes onto metal or presoaked wooden skewers, threading a cherry tomato between the pieces of fish. Transfer the kebabs to the grill (or grill pan), leaving at least 1 inch (2.5 cm) of space between the skewers. Sprinkle the fish and tomatoes with a little more salt. Cook, flipping halfway or more often if needed, until the fish is just barely cooked through and opaque, 5 to 8 minutes.

Transfer the kebabs to a platter, sprinkle with cilantro, squeeze the lime wedges over the fish, and serve.

Scallops Cooked on Rosemary Branches

Serves 6

Sturdy rosemary branches not only make a festive-looking serving tool, but they also impart skewered scallops with an extra dose of herby flavor. (Thank you to Suzanne Goin, who first showed me this trick!) The secret to browning scallops to burnished glory is to pat them completely dry before cooking them. You can serve these scallops as one of a few main dishes in a tapas-style meal. Or they make a lovely starter or side dish when you want to up the fanciness level, especially for a standing-room-only party.

18 sturdy rosemary branches, 3 inches (7.5 cm) long

Finely grated zest and juice of 1 lemon

18 large sea scallops

6 tablespoons (85 g) unsalted butter

Fine sea salt and freshly ground black pepper

Strip most of the leaves from the rosemary branches, leaving about 1 inch (2.5 cm) of leaves still attached to one end of each branch. Finely chop the stripped leaves and place in a small bowl along with the lemon zest. Cut the bare end of each branch to a sharp point.

Skewer one scallop onto each rosemary branch and place them on a sheet pan or large plate. Use paper towels to pat the scallops completely dry on all sides.

Heat a large stainless-steel skillet over medium-high heat for 1 minute. Working in batches, add 2 tablespoons of the butter and, once it has melted and starts to foam, place 6 scallops (or as many as will fit comfortably in a single layer without crowding) in the pan. Cook, without moving, until the bottoms are golden brown, 2 to 3 minutes. Flip the scallops, sprinkle generously with salt and pepper, and add one-third of the lemon juice. Cook until the scallops are just barely cooked through, 1 to 2 minutes. Transfer the scallops to a serving platter and pour the pan sauce over them. Repeat with the remaining butter and lemon juice to cook the remaining scallops.

Scatter the rosemary–lemon zest mixture on top and serve.

Kumquat-Crab Cakes with Dill Rémoulade

Serves 4

Crab cakes are a classic for a reason—they're easy to make and you can customize the mix-ins, using special regional ingredients like Creole mustard or a certain brand of saltine crackers. If you've never tried a kumquat, get ready to meet your new favorite citrus fruit. Kumquats look like tiny oranges. They taste as bright and refreshing as a chilled glass of grapefruit juice but they're sweet enough that you can even eat their zesty peel. In this crab cake recipe, the sweet-sour flavor of kumquats goes particularly well with dill-flecked rémoulade, a mayonnaise-based dipping sauce.

KUMQUAT-CRAB CAKES

1 large egg

½ cup (115 g) mayonnaise

1 tablespoon Creole mustard or whole-grain mustard

1 tablespoon Worcestershire sauce

1 tablespoon cornstarch

¼ teaspoon red pepper flakes

¼ teaspoon fine sea salt

1 pound (450 g) crabmeat, drained if needed, and picked over for any bits of shell

8 kumquats, thinly sliced and seeded

1 cup (70 g) crushed saltine crackers

½ cup (40 g) soft fresh bread crumbs

DILL RÉMOULADE

1 cup (225 g) mayonnaise

2 tablespoons Creole mustard or whole-grain mustard

½ cup (10 g) fresh dill, finely chopped

4 scallions, finely chopped

1 tablespoon fresh lemon juice

2 teaspoons paprika

TO FINISH

2 tablespoons extra-virgin olive oil

2 tablespoons unsalted butter

Lemon wedges, for serving

Make the kumquat-crab cakes: In a large bowl, combine the egg, mayonnaise, mustard, Worcestershire sauce, cornstarch, pepper flakes, and salt. Stir until smooth, then add the crabmeat, kumquats, and saltines. Use a rubber spatula to very gently fold everything together.

Divide the crab mixture into 8 equal portions. Shape them into cakes about ½ inch (1.3 cm) thick, dredge them in the bread crumbs, and place on a large plate or small sheet pan. Cover and refrigerate for at least 1 hour or up to overnight. ⟶

Make the dill rémoulade: In a medium bowl, combine the mayonnaise, mustard, dill, scallions, lemon juice, and paprika and stir well. Cover and refrigerate until ready to serve.

When you're ready to cook the crab cakes, in a heavy-bottomed skillet, heat the olive oil and butter over medium to medium-high heat. Add half the crab cakes to the pan and cook until golden brown and crisp on the first side, about 3 minutes. Gently flip and cook on the other side until nicely browned, 2 to 3 minutes more. Transfer to a warm plate and cook the remaining crab cakes. (The butter in the pan will have browned by now. That's okay—it's delicious!)

Serve the crab cakes warm, with the dill rémoulade and lemon wedges on the side.

Slow-Roasted Steelhead Trout with Shiso Salad

Serves 6 to 8

Steelhead trout looks and tastes a lot like salmon, but steelhead is usually a little more affordable on its native West Coast. When you're hosting parties, you'll often find yourself buying large quantities of ingredients, and things like seafood and meat can add up quickly, so look to the less expensive yet no less elegant options like steelhead (though you can use salmon in this recipe, if you prefer). The fish is topped with a salad made of thinly sliced Asian pear, Persian cucumber, and shiso leaves cut into ribbons. If you can't find shiso (also known as perilla), substitute with basil or mint—or a combo of both.

1 whole skin-on side of steelhead trout (2 to 3 pounds/0.9 to 1.4 kg)

2 tablespoons extra-virgin olive oil

Fine sea salt and freshly ground black pepper

SHISO SALAD

1 tablespoon plain whole-milk yogurt

1 tablespoon fresh lime juice

2 teaspoons rice vinegar

1 teaspoon honey

1 tablespoon white sesame seeds

1 small red chile pepper, seeded and finely chopped

1 scallion, sliced, white and green parts kept separate

Fine sea salt

1 Asian pear, cored and thinly sliced

2 Persian (mini) cucumbers, thinly sliced

6 red shiso leaves, sliced into thin ribbons

2 teaspoons toasted sesame oil

Preheat the oven to 250°F (120°C). Line a sheet pan with parchment paper.

Place the trout, skin side down, on the prepared sheet pan. Drizzle the olive oil over the fish and sprinkle generously with salt and pepper. Roast until flaky and just barely cooked in the center, 20 to 40 minutes, depending on the thickness.

While the fish roasts, make the shiso salad: In a medium bowl, whisk together the yogurt, lime juice, vinegar, honey, sesame seeds, chile pepper, scallion whites, and ½ teaspoon salt. Add the Asian pear and Persian cucumbers and toss gently with your hands until the pear and cucumbers are coated in the dressing. ⟶

Just before serving, add the shiso, sesame oil, and scallion greens to the salad and toss gently.

Transfer the trout to a serving platter. Pile the shiso salad directly on top of the fish and serve.

Do Ahead Most seafood doesn't reheat well and is really best served while still hot, but one exception is this slow-roasted trout. It tastes fantastic straight out of the oven and just as wonderful chilled. If you plan to serve it chilled, you can cook it up to 3 days ahead and store, covered, in the fridge. The dressing for the shiso salad can also be made up to 3 days ahead and stored in a jar in the fridge.

LINGERING FISHY SMELLS

We all want our homes to be welcoming, and fishy scents are . . . not ideal. But there are simple DIY remedies for this issue. One easy option is to leave out a bowl of white vinegar on the kitchen countertop. The vinegar will neutralize any questionable aromas. You can also simmer a small pot of water with any combination of lemon peels, bay leaves, and fresh rosemary sprigs for about 20 minutes (or, for a warmer scent, try cinnamon sticks, whole cloves, and/or slices of fresh ginger). A final solution is to leave out a bowl of coffee grounds or even just go ahead and brew some coffee, which always clears the air.

Winning Chili con Carne

Serves 6 to 8

Die-hard Texans will tell you that any self-respecting chili con carne doesn't have beans in it. That may be true as a regional tradition, but don't let that stop you from adding beans to your chili con carne to balance out the meatiness of the beef. Pintos are a delicious addition. This chili takes a couple of hours to cook until the meat is fork-tender, but the long cook time means this is an easy dish to make ahead and let simmer until your guests arrive.

4 large dried ancho chiles

1 teaspoon cumin seeds

2 teaspoons dried Mexican oregano

4 slices thick-cut bacon

1½ to 2 pounds (680 to 910 g) chuck beef, cut into 2-inch (5 cm) cubes

Fine sea salt

½ yellow onion, chopped

4 garlic cloves, thinly sliced

1 (12-ounce/360 ml) bottle dark beer

1 (28-ounce/795 g) can diced tomatoes

1 (15-ounce/425 g) can pinto beans (optional), drained and rinsed

FOR SERVING

½ yellow onion, finely chopped

Chopped fresh cilantro

Diced avocado

Tortilla chips

In a Dutch oven or heavy-bottomed stainless-steel pot, toast the ancho chiles over medium-high heat, flipping once, until floppy and fragrant, about 2 minutes. Transfer them to a plate. Add the cumin seeds to the pot and toast, stirring often, until the seeds begin to pop. Remove them from the pot.

Using a mortar and pestle or a spice grinder, grind the cumin seeds to a powder. Discard the stems and most of the seeds from the ancho chiles, and grind them to a powder. In a small bowl, combine the ground anchos, ground cumin seeds, and oregano and set aside.

Return the Dutch oven to medium heat. Add the bacon and cook, flipping, until browned and crisp, about 5 minutes. Use tongs to transfer the bacon to a plate, leaving the fat in the pot.

Increase the heat under the Dutch oven to medium-high and let the bacon fat heat up for 1 minute. Working in batches, add about one-third of the beef to the pan, sprinkle it with salt, and cook until dark brown on the undersides, 3 to 5 minutes. Turn and cook until nicely browned

on another side. Transfer the browned meat to a large plate and continue with the other batches.

Turn the heat down to medium and add the onion, garlic, and reserved spice mixture to the pot. Cook, stirring occasionally, until the onion is tender and golden brown, 8 to 10 minutes. Pour in the beer and diced tomatoes and use a wooden spoon to scrape the bottom of the pan to release any flavorful crusty bits. Return the browned meat to the pan, then pour in enough water to nearly but not quite cover the meat. Adjust the heat so that the liquid simmers gently. Cook, stirring occasionally, until the meat is fork-tender, 1 to 2 hours.

Use your hands to crumble the bacon and add that to the pot. If using beans, stir them in and let them warm up in the chili. Taste and season with more salt if needed.

Serve each bowl of chili topped with a sprinkling of chopped onion and cilantro, some avocado, and a handful of tortilla chips or let guests choose their own toppings.

Do Ahead Chili can be made up to 3 days ahead and stored, covered, in the fridge. Reheat over low heat on the stovetop, stirring occasionally. You can keep the chili warming on the stove for several hours so that it stays hot for your guests. Wait to garnish with the toppings until serving.

Bavette with Chimichurri

Serves 6

Chimichurri is a South American green sauce made from parsley, oregano, capers, and red wine vinegar. It complements steak so well that once you try the two together, you'll want to eat steak only with chimichurri ever again. For parties, the sauce can be made ahead, but try to cook the steak as close to serving time as you can. You can do it either in a ripping-hot cast-iron skillet on the stovetop or outdoors on a grill (see Note).

2 pounds (910 g) bavette steak, flank steak, or skirt steak

Fine sea salt and freshly ground black pepper

CHIMICHURRI

3 garlic cloves, peeled but whole

2 tablespoons capers, rinsed

2 bunches fresh flat-leaf parsley, tough bottom stems trimmed

2 tablespoons fresh oregano leaves

2 tablespoons red wine vinegar, plus more to taste

Finely grated zest and juice of 1 lemon

1 teaspoon fine sea salt, plus more to taste

Freshly ground black pepper

¾ cup (180 ml) extra-virgin olive oil

TO FINISH

2 tablespoons olive oil

4 tablespoons (½ stick/55 g) unsalted butter, fridge-cold

Generously season both sides of the steak with salt and pepper. Let the steak rest at room temperature for at least 15 minutes.

Meanwhile, make the chimichurri: In a food processor, combine the garlic, capers, parsley, oregano, vinegar, lemon zest, lemon juice, salt, and lots of pepper and process until the parsley and oregano are finely chopped. You may need to stop the machine and scrape down the sides a couple of times. Add the olive oil and process to combine. Taste, adding more salt if needed. The chimichurri should taste balanced between sharp from the vinegar and smooth from the oil; if it's oilier than you'd like, stir in another splash of vinegar.

To finish: Heat a large cast-iron skillet over medium-high heat for 3 to 4 minutes, until it's so hot it's nearly smoking. Use paper towels to pat the steak completely dry. Cut the steak into two pieces. Swirl 1 tablespoon of the olive oil into the pan. Place one piece of steak in the skillet and cook until browned on the first side, about 4 minutes. Flip and cook on the second side to your preferred doneness, 3 to 5 minutes

for medium-rare, depending on the thickness. (If using a thermometer to check for doneness, 135ºF (57ºC) is medium-rare and 145ºF (63ºC) is medium.)

Transfer the steak to a plate, place half the butter on top, and let rest for about 5 minutes. Meanwhile, repeat to cook the other steak piece.

Slice the steak against the grain and arrange the slices on a serving platter. Drizzle any melted butter and juices from the cut steak over the top and serve the chimichurri in a bowl alongside.

Note If you'd like to grill the steak, light your grill and heat to high. Brush the grill grates clean, then dip a folded piece of paper towel in olive oil and use tongs to rub it across the grill. Use paper towels to pat the steak completely dry. Drizzle lightly with oil on both sides. Place the steak on the grill diagonally across the grill grates. Cook until browned on the underside, about 3 minutes. Flip and cook on the second side to your preferred doneness, another 3 minutes or so for medium-rare. (If using a thermometer to check for doneness, 135°F (57°C) is medium-rare and 145°F (63°C) is medium.) Serve the steak as directed in the recipe.

Brisket and Harissa Buttered Carrots

Serves 8 to 10

The secret to making the perfect meltingly tender and flavorful brisket is to use both the grill (for high heat) and the oven (for low heat). First, some time on a hot grill will give the meat a delicious smokiness. Then a long and slow roast in a low oven turns the meat fork-tender. Plan for about 1 hour of grilling time followed by at least 9 hours of roasting time. If you're comfortable leaving your oven on overnight, that's a great chance for the brisket to roast to melting doneness. Otherwise, plan to grill first thing in the morning and then pop the meat in the oven for the long and slow cook as you go about your day. And don't worry if you do not have a grill—there's a little work-around trick for using only an oven (see Note).

BRISKET

6 tablespoons (80 g) brown sugar

3 tablespoons fine sea salt

3 tablespoons freshly ground black pepper

3 tablespoons smoked paprika

2 tablespoons za'atar

1 beef brisket (10 to 12 pounds/4.5 to 5.4 kg)

2 cups (180 g) wood chips, soaked in water for at least 30 minutes

CARROTS

2 bunches carrots (about 1 pound/ 450 g total), greens trimmed, scrubbed but not peeled

4 tablespoons (½ stick/55 g) unsalted butter

¼ cup (60 ml) extra-virgin olive oil

2 garlic cloves, minced

½ teaspoon fine sea salt

3 tablespoons harissa

Prepare the brisket: The evening before you'd like to serve the brisket, or early the morning of, in a small bowl, stir together the brown sugar, salt, pepper, smoked paprika, and za'atar. Rub this spice mixture all over the brisket, massaging it gently into the meat. Let the meat rest at room temperature while you prepare the grill.

For a gas grill, heat one side to high. For a charcoal grill, build a fire under a basket of charcoal, and when the coals are ready, mound them on one side of the grill to create a hot side and a cooler side. Place the brisket, fat side up, on the cooler side of the grill and add half of the soaked wood chips to the hot side. Cover the grill and cook for about 20 minutes. Flip the brisket, add the remaining soaked wood chips, and continue grilling for another 20 minutes. →

Transfer the brisket, fat side up again, to a large piece of heavy-duty aluminum foil. Wrap tightly and place in a roasting pan large enough to fit the wrapped brisket comfortably. Preheat the oven to 225°F (110°C) and roast the brisket until very tender, about 9 hours or overnight.

When ready to serve, unwrap the brisket and save all the juices in the pan. On a cutting board, thinly slice the brisket across the grain, then return the slices to the pan of juices and mix to redistribute them.

Prepare the carrots: Thinly slice them crosswise into coins. In a large skillet, combine the butter and olive oil and warm over medium-high heat. Once the butter has melted, add the garlic, sliced carrots, and salt. Cook, stirring occasionally, until the carrots are just barely tender, about 4 minutes. Remove the skillet from the heat and mix in the harissa.

Serve the brisket and harissa buttered carrots together.

Note If you don't have a grill, you can achieve the desired smoky flavor using your oven. Preheat the broiler to high and position the rack directly below the heating element. Place the brisket, fat side up, on a sheet pan. Broil it until some dark brown marks appear on top, moving the brisket as needed. Flip and broil on the other side until browned in a few places. The total broiling time ranges from 10 to 20 minutes, depending on the strength of your broiler (they vary widely!).

Do Ahead Grill the brisket, wrap in foil, and roast as directed. Unwrap the cooked brisket from its foil packet but wait to cut it. Let it cool to room temperature in its juices and then transfer to the fridge to chill for up to 3 days. When you're ready to serve, slice the brisket, return the slices to the juices, and reheat gently in a 200°F (90°C) oven, stirring once or twice, until hot all the way through, about 10 minutes.

Variation

BRISKET SANDWICHES

If you'd rather serve this dish as finger food, slice the brisket into smaller pieces and arrange them on a platter, alongside soft, squishy slider buns, some pickles, and a bowl of red cabbage slaw (simply slice red cabbage as thinly as you can manage and season with freshly squeezed lemon juice, the tiniest drizzle of extra-virgin olive oil, and salt to taste). You could opt to skip the harissa carrots or, if you'd like, try tossing them in with the cabbage for a slightly spicy slaw.

Roasted Chickens and Schmaltzy-Oven Potatoes

Serves 8

Two beautifully roasted whole chickens might seem like a fancy party trick, but the secret is that roasting two chickens at the same time is just as easy as roasting one. For even a medium-size party, you'll likely want two chickens to make sure everyone is well fed. The chicken schmaltz that's released while the birds roast is delicious and makes the best fat to coat oven-roasted potatoes that you can cook and serve alongside. It's a two-in-one, twice!

Fine sea salt

1 tablespoon paprika

2 teaspoons freshly ground
  black pepper

1 teaspoon dried oregano

2 small whole chickens (3½ to
  4 pounds/1.6 to 1.8 kg each)

3 pounds (1.4 kg) baby potatoes

In a small bowl, stir together 2½ tablespoons salt and the paprika, pepper, and oregano. Season the chickens all over and on the insides with the spice blend. Place the chickens side by side in a roasting pan. Turn the wing tips under and secure them under the bird so they don't burn in the oven. Cover loosely and refrigerate for at least 3 hours or up to 2 days.

Remove the chickens from the refrigerator and let them come to room temperature, at least 1 hour and up to 3 hours before roasting.

About 15 minutes before you're ready to roast the chickens, preheat the oven to 450°F (230°C).

Roast the chickens for 30 minutes.

Meanwhile, bring a medium saucepan of generously salted water to a boil. Add the potatoes and cook until tender when poked with a fork, 15 to 20 minutes. Drain in a colander, then return the potatoes to the empty, still-hot pan and shake them around to burst some of them open. Transfer them to a roasting dish large enough that they fit snugly in a single layer.

Remove the chickens from the oven and use a sturdy spatula to hold the chickens in place while you tilt the dish over the potatoes, allowing the schmaltz and juices to drizzle. Stir the potatoes around until well

coated. Return the chickens in their pan to the oven and place the potatoes in their dish on the rack alongside the chickens.

Roast until the potatoes are crisp and browned in a few places and the chickens are amber brown and cooked through, another 30 minutes or so. Check for doneness by wiggling the chicken legs—they should move freely and feel a little loose in the joint. You can also cut the skin between the breast and thigh to see if the juices run clear.

Carve the chickens and serve the schmaltzy-oven potatoes alongside.

TO TRUSS OR NOT TO TRUSS CHICKEN?

You know that fancy-looking technique for tying up chicken, turkey, and other roasted birds? There's a proper cooking school way to do it, of course, one that involves finding the neck bone and doing a cat's-cradle game of hooking twine around it. The main idea is to bring all the loose limbs inward toward the center, creating a compact mass that will roast more evenly in the oven. But you might be wondering if it's absolutely necessary to truss. What if you don't have butcher's twine at home? Don't worry, you can roast chicken without trussing—it'll turn out wonderfully. The key is generously seasoning it with more salt than you think it needs and some complementary spices, like the paprika and dried oregano used in the recipe above. If you do happen to have some twine, you can consider simply tying the chicken's legs together, which requires only one regular knot and will make the roasted bird look a little more special for guests.

Potato Chip–Crust Chicken with Green Olive Relish

Serves 6 to 8

Your new favorite chicken recipe. If you're Team Salt-and-Vinegar Chips or a lover of all things salty, sour, and briny, this one is for you. Crushed salt-and-vinegar potato chips get boosted with fresh herbs and cheese to make a flavor-packed coating to bread the chicken, and as a bonus, they're also gluten-free friendly. Cooking breaded chicken in the oven is as easy as can be—no need to worry about panfrying or deep-frying here.

CHICKEN

1 (8.5-ounce/240 g) bag salt-and-vinegar potato chips

½ cup (50 g) freshly grated Parmigiano-Reggiano cheese

¼ cup (5 g) fresh dill, chopped

¼ cup (5 g) fresh flat-leaf parsley, chopped

½ bunch (5 g) fresh chives, chopped

3 large eggs

2 tablespoons whole milk

Fine sea salt and freshly ground black pepper

3 pounds (1.4 kg) boneless, skinless chicken (either breasts or thighs or even a combo)

RELISH

3 garlic cloves, peeled but whole

2 tablespoons capers, rinsed

2 bunches fresh flat-leaf parsley, tough bottom stems trimmed

2 tablespoons red wine vinegar

Finely grated zest and juice of 1 lemon

1 teaspoon fine sea salt

Freshly ground black pepper

¾ cup (180 ml) extra-virgin olive oil

1 cup (180 g) Castelvetrano olives, pitted and coarsely chopped

Preheat the oven to 400°F (200°C). Line a sheet pan with parchment paper.

Prepare the chicken: Crush the potato chips in their bag until they're the texture of fine bread crumbs. Place them in a wide shallow bowl and stir in the Parmigiano, dill, parsley, and chives. In a second wide shallow bowl, whisk the eggs, milk, a pinch of salt, and a few grinds of pepper.

Pat the chicken pieces dry with paper towels, sprinkle them with salt, and cut into 2-inch (5 cm) pieces. If they're not thinner than ½ inch (1.3 cm), pound them with a meat mallet or rolling pin until they are. Dip each piece first in the egg mixture and then in the chip mixture, rolling to coat all sides evenly. Place the coated chicken pieces in a

single layer on the prepared sheet pan. Bake until golden brown on the undersides, about 20 minutes. Flip and bake until cooked through, 5 to 15 minutes more.

Meanwhile, make the relish: In a food processor, combine the garlic, capers, parsley, vinegar, lemon zest, lemon juice, salt, and lots of pepper. Blend until the parsley is finely chopped. Add the olive oil and blend until incorporated. Transfer the mixture to a serving bowl and stir in the olives.

Serve the chicken hot from the oven, with the green olive relish on the side or dolloped artfully on top.

Do Ahead If you'd like to get ahead, you can prepare the chicken up to the step before baking, cover it, and refrigerate for up to 2 days. About 30 minutes before you'd like to serve the chicken, proceed with the recipe. The relish can be made up to 4 days ahead and stored in an airtight container in the fridge.

Herby Turkey Meatballs

Serves 6

Meatballs baked in sauce are a perfect main dish all on their own, of course, but you can always serve them with a side of pasta for a larger feast. Turkey meatballs are a lighter option than pork or beef balls. They come together quickly and can be made ahead. Save some time by looking for a jar of good-quality marinara sauce at the grocery store or an Italian market. But don't skip the fresh herbs in this recipe or substitute with dried herbs. The fresh herb leaves melt into the meat mixture like woven threads of flavor.

1 pound (450 g) ground turkey

2 garlic cloves, minced

1 small bunch fresh flat-leaf parsley, finely chopped

½ cup (10 g) fresh basil leaves, finely chopped

¼ cup (5 g) fresh mint leaves, finely chopped

¾ cup (185 g) whole-milk ricotta cheese

½ cup (50 g) freshly grated Parmigiano-Reggiano cheese

1 teaspoon fine sea salt

Freshly ground black pepper

3 tablespoons extra-virgin olive oil

1 (28-ounce/795 g) jar good-quality marinara sauce

3 sprigs fresh oregano

Preheat the oven to 425ºF (220ºC).

In a large bowl, combine the turkey, garlic, parsley, basil, mint, ricotta, Parmigiano, salt, and lots of black pepper. Mix well to combine (your hands are really the best tool for this step—they will help distribute the seasoning evenly throughout the meat). Shape into about 20 meatballs that are a little smaller than golf balls and place them in a 9 by 13-inch (23 by 33 cm) baking dish. Drizzle with the oil.

Roast in the oven, shaking the dish once or twice to turn the meatballs, until browned, about 20 minutes.

Turn down the oven temperature to 375ºF (190ºC). Pour the marinara sauce over the meatballs, scatter the oregano sprigs on top, and return the dish to the oven to continue roasting until the sauce is heated through and bubbling, 15 minutes or so.

To serve, stick a toothpick or short skewer into each meatball still in the baking dish. Place the dish in the middle of the table and serve while the meatballs are hot and juicy.

Yakitori-Style Tsukune Sauced with Ume Plum Tare

Serves 8

Tsukune are grilled ground-chicken skewers that are served at yakitori restaurants. In this version, the tsukune take the shape of a classic spherical meatball, which is a little easier to cook at home in the oven. You can make them any size you like. Small, one-bite balls would be ideal for a standing-room-only party, and larger, golf-ball-size meatballs are better for seated meals. Salty umeboshi are pickled ume (fruits that are closely related to plums and apricots), and they are traditionally served as a side dish or with steamed rice, but they're way too tasty not to use in other ways. Try cooking ume plum jam and ume plum vinegar into a dark tare-style sauce (see Note) that's wonderful brushed on the chicken meatballs and served as a dipping sauce alongside. If you can't find the ume ingredients, just use regular plum jam and rice vinegar or black vinegar and be sure to taste the sauce for saltiness—you may need to add a bit more soy sauce.

UME PLUM TARE

¾ cup (180 ml) mirin

½ cup (120 ml) soy sauce or tamari

¼ cup packed (55 g) brown sugar

¼ cup (80 g) ume plum jam

¼ cup (60 g) pickled ginger, drained

1 tablespoon ume plum vinegar

1 tablespoon cornstarch plus
   1 tablespoon water mixed to
   form a slurry

TSUKUNE

Vegetable oil, for the sheet pan

2 pounds (910 g) ground chicken,
   preferably thigh meat

1 bunch scallions, finely chopped

2 large eggs

½ cup (30 g) panko bread crumbs

1 (2-inch/5 cm) piece fresh ginger,
   peeled and finely grated

4 garlic cloves, finely grated

1 tablespoon toasted sesame oil

1½ teaspoons fine sea salt

Make the ume plum tare: In a small saucepan, combine the mirin, soy sauce, brown sugar, jam, pickled ginger, and vinegar. Bring to a boil and then adjust the heat so that the mixture simmers. Cook until reduced in volume enough to coat the back of a spoon, about 20 minutes. Stir in the cornstarch slurry and cook for 1 minute. Strain the sauce through a fine-mesh sieve and set aside or refrigerate in an airtight container for up to 3 days.

Make the tsukune: Preheat the oven to 400°F (200°C). Line a sheet pan with aluminum foil and drizzle vegetable oil on the foil. →

In a large bowl, combine the ground chicken, scallions, eggs, panko, grated ginger, garlic, sesame oil, and salt. Mix thoroughly to combine. Using wet hands, shape the mixture into meatballs about the size of golf balls and space them out on the prepared sheet pan.

Bake until browned on the undersides, 10 to 15 minutes. Use tongs to turn the meatballs on the sheet pan. Brush them generously with the ume plum tare sauce, and return to the oven to bake until cooked through, 3 to 5 minutes.

Transfer the meatballs to a warm platter, brush with any leftover sauce, and serve.

Note Tare is a thick, sweet soy sauce that packs an umami punch.

Slow-Cooked Pork in Cabbage Leaf Cups

Serves 6 to 8

The most tender and juicy pork is achieved by roasting the meat for a very long time at a relatively low temperature. Toasting whole spices for a spice rub and letting the meat marinate overnight infuses the pork with maximum flavor. And when you're ready to cook the pork, the oven does all the hard work. A large roast like this makes it easy to stretch for a crowd and is sure to please any guest, especially when served with quick-pickled red onion, tangy BBQ sauce, and cabbage leaf cups.

ROASTED PORK

1 tablespoon black peppercorns

2 teaspoons cumin seeds

¼ cup (70 g) fine sea salt

¼ cup packed (55 g) brown sugar

7 pounds (3.2 kg) bone-in, skin-on pork shoulder

BBQ SAUCE

⅔ cup (180 g) ketchup

⅓ cup (80 ml) apple cider vinegar

¼ cup packed (55 g) brown sugar

2 teaspoons sweet or hot smoked paprika

1 teaspoon freshly ground black pepper

FOR SERVING

1 small red onion

3 limes

Fine sea salt

1 small head cabbage, leaves separated and torn into cups

Prepare the roasted pork: In a small dry skillet, toast the peppercorns and cumin seeds over medium heat, shaking the pan often, until fragrant, about 1 minute. Transfer to a mortar and pestle and crush to a powder. Mix in the salt and brown sugar.

Place the pork on a quarter-sheet pan or in a roasting pan of similar size (13 by 9 inches/33 by 23 cm). Rub the spice mixture over the pork on all sides. Cover with plastic wrap and refrigerate overnight. (If you're short on time, let the meat rest at room temperature for an hour or two.)

About 15 minutes before you're ready to cook the pork, preheat the oven to 300°F (150°C).

Remove the plastic and position the pork so that it is skin side up. Roast until pull-apart tender when poked with a fork, 6 to 7 hours.

Meanwhile, make the BBQ sauce: In a small stainless-steel saucepan, combine the ketchup, vinegar, brown sugar, smoked paprika, and black pepper. Bring to a gentle simmer over medium heat and cook, stirring occasionally, until darker in color, about 10 minutes.

Let the roasted pork rest for about 30 minutes, then transfer it to a cutting board and use two forks to pull it apart and shred it. Add half of the BBQ sauce to the pork and mix well. Save the rest of the sauce for serving.

When almost ready to serve: Slice the red onion as thinly as possible and place in a bowl. Add the finely grated zest of 2 limes and squeeze in the juice of all 3 limes. Season with a few pinches of salt. Set aside until the onion softens, about 5 minutes.

Serve the pork, reserved BBQ sauce, pickled onions, and cabbage leaves all together and let everyone assemble their own cups by spooning some pork and sauce into a cabbage leaf and topping with a tangle of pickled onions.

Do Ahead The BBQ sauce can be made up to 2 weeks ahead and stored in an airtight container in the fridge. (You can also just use store-bought sauce.) Get ahead by making the pork all the way through the step where you mix in half of the BBQ sauce. Cover and refrigerate for up to 3 days. To reheat the pork, warm it gently in a 200°F (90°C) oven, stirring once or twice, until hot all the way through, about 10 minutes.

Tacos al Pastor

Serves 6 to 8

The pork for al pastor tacos is marinated in a fragrant combination of dried chile peppers, onion, garlic, and spices like cumin and oregano. It would probably be delicious to stop right there, but al pastor has one additional genius ingredient: pineapple. The fruit tenderizes the meat and flavors it simultaneously. Another traditional ingredient in al pastor is annatto, a ground spice made from the seeds of the achiote tree, and the earthy, sweet, and faintly floral scent adds another layer of flavor to the meat. Look for annatto in Mexican markets, but don't worry if you can't find it. The dish will still be delicious without it. Proper al pastor meat is cooked on a vertical rotisserie called a trompo. As the meat browns, it is shaved off and nestled in warm tortillas for tacos. Having a trompo would no doubt lead to a smashing success of a party, but just in case you'd like to make al pastor using your stovetop and oven, this recipe will show you how.

2 pounds (910 g) pork tenderloin

2 dried guajillo chiles

1 large white onion

4 garlic cloves, peeled but whole

1 plum tomato, cut into quarters

5 tablespoons (75 ml) vegetable oil

3 tablespoons brown sugar

2 tablespoons fresh lime juice

1 teaspoon cumin seeds

1 teaspoon dried Mexican oregano

½ teaspoon ground achiote seeds (annatto)

1 (20-ounce/570 g) can juice-packed pineapple slices, drained

Fine sea salt

2 tablespoons honey

FOR SERVING

18 corn tortillas, warmed over a gas flame

Very finely chopped white onion

Chopped fresh cilantro

Lime wedges

Place the pork in a large ziplock bag and chill in the freezer for 1 hour. (Once the meat is semi-frozen and firm, it'll be much easier to slice.)

Meanwhile, remove the stems from the chiles and shake out most of the seeds. In a small, dry saucepan, toast the chiles over medium-high heat, flipping once, until floppy and fragrant, about 2 minutes. Pour in enough hot water to barely cover, bring to a simmer, then cover and remove from the heat. Let soak for at least 15 minutes or up to 1 hour. Use tongs to transfer the soaked chiles to a food processor. (Discard the soaking liquid.) ⟶

Remove the pork from the freezer, place it on a clean cutting board, and cut across the grain into slices as thin as possible, ideally less than ⅛ inch (3 mm) thick. Return the pork to the bag and set aside while you prepare the marinade.

Coarsely chop half of the onion and place it in the food processor with the soaked chiles. Add the garlic, tomato, 3 tablespoons of the vegetable oil, the brown sugar, lime juice, cumin seeds, oregano, achiote, half of the pineapple, and 1 tablespoon salt. Blend until pureed.

Pour this marinade into the bag with the pork. Thinly slice the remaining half of the onion and add it to the bag with the sliced pork. Gently squeeze the bag to mix well. Refrigerate for at least 30 minutes or up to 24 hours.

In a large stainless-steel skillet, heat 1 tablespoon of the vegetable oil over high heat for 2 minutes. Add about half of the pork and marinade from the bag to the pan. Cook, stirring occasionally, until the liquid evaporates and the meat browns around the edges, about 20 minutes. Transfer to a serving platter. Wipe out the pan and repeat to cook the remaining pork.

Meanwhile, heat the oven broiler to high. Arrange the remaining pineapple in a single layer on a sheet pan. Brush with the honey. Place under the broiler and cook, rotating the sheet pan as needed to promote even browning, until dark brown in a few places, 5 to 10 minutes.

To serve: Place the pork platter on the table along with the broiled pineapple, warm tortillas, chopped onion, cilantro, and lime wedges. Serve right away.

Bánh Bagnat Mì with Lemongrass Tofu

Serves 4 to 6

What do you get when you mash up French pan bagnat and Vietnamese bánh mì? Bánh bagnat mì, of course—a party-size sandwich generously filled with lemongrass tofu and pickled vegetables (inspired by my go-to bánh mì order) that gets wrapped and pressed by a heavy weight in the style of pan bagnat. This sandwich is one big vegetarian main course, perfect for an outdoor party like Pack-and-Go Picnic! (page 281). Make it vegan by using vegan mayonnaise.

LEMONGRASS TOFU

3 stalks lemongrass

4 garlic cloves

4 scallions, coarsely chopped

1 (2-inch/5 cm) piece fresh ginger, peeled and finely grated

1 small serrano chile, seeded and coarsely chopped

Finely grated zest and juice of 2 limes

1 bunch fresh cilantro, lower stems trimmed

Fine sea salt

1 (13.5-ounce/400 ml) can full-fat coconut milk

1 (14-ounce/400 g) package extra-firm tofu, cut into ½-inch (1.3 cm) slabs

PICKLED VEGETABLES

¾ cup (85 g) shredded daikon radish

¾ cup (85 g) shredded carrots

½ cucumber, thinly sliced

2 tablespoons rice vinegar

2 tablespoons sugar

¼ teaspoon fine sea salt

FOR ASSEMBLY

⅓ cup (75 g) mayonnaise (or vegan mayo, if you like)

1 tablespoon sriracha

1 (16-inch/40 cm) loaf Vietnamese-style soft bread or ciabatta

1 bunch fresh mint, leaves picked

1 jalapeño, thinly sliced

Prepare the lemongrass tofu: Trim off and discard all but the bottom few inches of the lemongrass stalks. Peel away the fibrous green layers until you reach the softer white-purple interior. Chop coarsely and place in a food processor. Add the garlic, scallions, ginger, serrano, lime zest, lime juice, half the cilantro, and ¾ teaspoon salt. Blend to a paste.

Heat a saucepan over medium-high heat. Open the can of coconut milk and spoon into the pan the thick, creamy part that has risen to the top. Add the lemongrass paste and cook, stirring often, for a few minutes. Pour in the remaining coconut milk and bring to a simmer, then remove from the heat. ⟶

Place the tofu in a dish large enough to accommodate the slabs in a single layer. Pour in the lemongrass sauce. Let marinate at room temperature for at least 15 minutes or up to 3 days in the refrigerator.

Meanwhile, make the pickled vegetables: In a bowl, toss together the daikon, carrots, cucumber, vinegar, sugar, and salt. Let pickle at room temperature for at least 15 minutes or up to 3 days in the refrigerator.

To assemble: In a small bowl, stir together the mayonnaise and sriracha.

Slice the bread in half lengthwise, leaving it hinged on one side. Toast for a few minutes under a broiler, if you like. Spread some of the lemongrass marinade on the bottom side of the loaf and spread the sriracha mayonnaise on the top side. Tile the lemongrass tofu on top of the lemongrass marinade and top with the pickled vegetables, mint, jalapeño, and remaining cilantro.

Close the sandwich, firmly pressing it together, and wrap it tightly first in parchment and then in foil. Place in the refrigerator and balance a heavy cast-iron skillet on top to weight down the sandwich for at least 1 hour and up to 24 hours before serving.

Vegetarian Nachos with Sweet Potato, Pintos en Adobo, and Cotija

Serves 6 to 8

Nachos are a classic party food and for good reason. They're snackable (ideal for eating while watching the big game) and shareable. These vegetarian nachos are layered with all kinds of delicious ingredients but come together quickly.

1½ pounds (680 g) tomatoes

½ pound (225 g) tomatillos, husked

4 garlic cloves, peeled but whole

3 dried chiles de arbol, stemmed

1 small bunch fresh cilantro, bottom stems trimmed, plus more for serving

1 teaspoon cumin seeds

Fine sea salt

1 large sweet potato, peeled and diced

1 (15-ounce/425 g) can pinto beans, drained and rinsed

2 canned chipotle peppers in adobo sauce, plus 1 tablespoon adobo sauce

1 (12-ounce/340 g) bag tortilla chips

1½ cups (170 g) shredded Monterey Jack cheese

1½ cups (170 g) shredded white cheddar cheese

4 radishes, thinly sliced

1 pint (12 ounces/340 g) cherry tomatoes, halved

1 large or 2 small avocados, sliced

½ cup (50 g) pickled jalapeños, drained

½ cup (60 g) crumbled Cotija cheese or queso fresco

Lime wedges, for serving

In a medium saucepan, combine the whole tomatoes, whole tomatillos, garlic, and chiles de arbol. Pour in enough hot water to comfortably submerge and bring to a rapid simmer. Cook until the tomatoes and chiles are puffy, about 10 minutes.

Use a slotted spoon to transfer the cooked tomatoes, tomatillos, garlic, and chiles to a blender. (Reserve the saucepan and cooking liquid.) Add the cilantro, cumin seeds, and 1 teaspoon salt to the blender and puree until mostly smooth. Set the tomato/tomatillo salsa aside.

Preheat the oven to 425°F (220°C).

Add the sweet potato to the cooking water in the saucepan and bring to a simmer. Cook until the sweet potato is tender when poked with a fork, about 10 minutes. Drain. →

Rinse out the saucepan, pour in the tomato/tomatillo salsa, and bring to a gentle simmer. Cook, stirring occasionally, until slightly thickened and darkened in color, about 10 minutes.

In a medium bowl, combine the pinto beans, chipotle peppers, and adobo sauce. Using a fork, stir well and mash some of the beans.

Spread about one-third of the tortilla chips across a sheet pan. Top with about one-third of the salsa, pintos en adobo, and sweet potato. Scatter handfuls of the Monterey Jack and cheddar cheeses over everything. Top with another layer of tortilla chips, salsa, pintos en adobo, sweet potato, and shredded cheeses. Make one final layer.

Bake until the cheeses have melted, 10 to 12 minutes.

Top the cooked nachos with the radishes, cherry tomatoes, avocado, pickled jalapeños, and Cotija. Serve hot, sprinkled with fresh cilantro, with lime wedges on the side for squeezing.

EDIBLE AND INTERACTIVE CENTERPIECES (AKA SNACK-TIVITIES)

Snack-tivities are foods that ask you to put in a little bit of active work while you're enjoying them—a snack and an activity in one. Guests tend to love keeping their hands busy by mindlessly working away at removing a tangerine peel in one piece or cracking peanut shells. Some snack-tivities are messier than others, and it's probably best to skip pomegranate shelling at the party table. (Do that in the kitchen, where clothing stains are less likely and cleanup is more manageable.) But there are plenty of interactive foods that you can set on the table as edible centerpieces. Some favorite party snack-tivities include a bowl of tangerines (look for the ones with their pretty green leaves still attached) for peeling, walnuts in the shell and a nutcracker, and pears or apples (or a combo) for slicing arranged on a tower or cake stand. Other nuts like pistachios and peanuts are great, and so, too, are sunflower seeds. Pomelo peeling can get a little juicy and is fantastic to do with friends, although it might not be ideal for the fanciest party. A fancy snack-tivity would be cracking the claws and prying out succulent meat from Dungeness crab or lobster—ooh la la! (Shout-out to my cousin Harper for coming up with the name "Snack-tivities.")

Squash Blossom and Sweet Pepper Tart

Serves 6 to 8

This tart is an ode to peak summer, with sweet Jimmy Nardello peppers and fresh squash blossoms. You can find both at farmers' markets in August. The colors are gorgeous, and best of all, this tart is super easy to make because it relies on a store-bought puff pastry. Look for the kind made with 100 percent butter. (Trader Joe's sells a great one.) It'll keep well in your freezer for months.

2 sheets frozen puff pastry (from one 18.3-ounce/520 g package)

6 ounces (170 g) soft goat cheese, crumbled

½ cup (120 ml) plus 1 tablespoon heavy cream

Fine sea salt and freshly ground black pepper

2 tablespoons extra-virgin olive oil

1 pound (450 g) Jimmy Nardello peppers or other sweet peppers, stemmed and thinly sliced

1 tablespoon red wine vinegar or sherry vinegar

2 tablespoons fresh oregano leaves, finely chopped

8 large squash blossoms

1 large egg

¼ cup (25 g) freshly grated Parmigiano-Reggiano cheese

Position racks in the top and center of the oven and preheat the oven to 425°F (220°C). Line two sheet pans with parchment paper.

Remove the puff pastry from the freezer and let it thaw for a few minutes. When it has thawed enough to be unfolded, place one sheet on each of the prepared sheet pans.

In a large bowl, combine the goat cheese, ½ cup (120 ml) of the cream, ¼ teaspoon salt, and a few grinds of black pepper. Stir vigorously with a wooden spoon until well blended.

Heat a large cast-iron skillet over medium-high heat for 1 minute. Add the olive oil and sweet peppers, stir to coat the peppers in the oil, and cook, without stirring, until the peppers are dark brown in a few places, about 3 minutes. Stir, then cook, stirring only once or twice, until the peppers are tender, about 5 minutes. Transfer the peppers to a bowl and mix in the vinegar, oregano, and ¼ teaspoon salt. ⟶

Use the tip of a small knife to score a border 1 inch (2.5 cm) in from the edge of each puff pastry. Divide the goat cheese mixture evenly between the two pastry sheets and spread it evenly, staying within the border.

Arrange the cooked peppers on top of the cheese, then gently nestle the squash blossoms among the peppers.

In a small bowl, beat the egg with the remaining 1 tablespoon cream. Brush the egg mixture over the exposed pastry border on both tarts, then sprinkle the edges with the Parmigiano.

Bake until the crusts are puffed and deep golden brown, about 20 minutes, switching racks and rotating the sheets front to back about halfway through.

Let cool for about 5 minutes before slicing and serving.

Furikake Kabocha Moons

Serves 8

The Japanese seasoning blend called furikake—made up of finely chopped dried seaweed, sesame seeds, sugar, and salt—is like magic dust. It adds a boost of umami to anything it touches. Traditionally it's sprinkled on rice, but it is also wonderful here on roasted kabocha squash. A simple ginger-sesame dressing brings the squash to another level, and avocado and mizuna leaves add textural interest.

2 small or 1 large kabocha squash

3 tablespoons untoasted sesame oil or vegetable oil

2 tablespoons furikake

1 (1-inch/2.5 cm) piece fresh ginger, peeled and finely grated

2 garlic cloves, finely grated

¼ cup (60 ml) rice vinegar

3 tablespoons toasted sesame oil

2 tablespoons tahini

1 tablespoon soy sauce or tamari

1 tablespoon warm water

2 teaspoons honey

3 cups (60 g) mizuna leaves, baby mustard greens, or baby spinach

3 avocados, cut into thick wedges

Steamed rice, for serving

Preheat the oven to 425°F (220°C). Line two sheet pans with parchment paper.

Place the whole squash in the oven directly on the rack to warm for 10 minutes, which will make it easier to slice.

Cut the squash in half, scoop out and discard the seeds and stringy bits, and cut into wedges 1 inch (2.5 cm) thick. Place them, cut side down, on the prepared sheet pans. Drizzle with the untoasted sesame oil and sprinkle with the furikake.

Roast until tender and browned around the edges, about 25 minutes, flipping the wedges and switching the position of the sheets on the racks about halfway through.

Meanwhile, in a small bowl, stir together the ginger, garlic, and vinegar. Let rest for about 5 minutes to allow the garlic flavor to mellow. Whisk in the toasted sesame oil, tahini, soy sauce, warm water, and honey.

Arrange the roasted kabocha on a platter with the mizuna leaves and avocado wedges, artfully layering the components. Drizzle the ginger-sesame dressing over everything. Serve with rice.

Crunchy-Topped Mac 'n' Squash

Serves 6 to 8

Mac 'n' cheese but make it vegetable-forward. This pasta dish has pureed butternut squash mixed in for an extra dose of orange color and some smooth creaminess without the cream. Trust me when I say your guests will be asking for this recipe.

1 butternut squash (about 2 pounds/ 910 g), peeled and cut into ¾-inch (2 cm) cubes

3 cups (710 ml) whole milk

1 sprig fresh sage

Fine sea salt

1 pound (450 g) shell or elbow pasta

1 cup (55 g) panko bread crumbs

4 tablespoons (½ stick/115 g) unsalted butter, melted

1 tablespoon fresh oregano leaves

1 tablespoon fresh thyme leaves

Finely grated zest of 1 lemon

1½ cups (170 g) shredded sharp cheddar cheese

½ cup (50 g) freshly grated Pecorino Romano cheese

Freshly ground black pepper

Preheat the oven to 375°F (190°C).

In a medium saucepan, combine the squash, milk, sage, and 1 teaspoon salt and bring to a simmer. Partially cover the pot and cook until the squash is tender when poked with a fork, 15 to 20 minutes.

Meanwhile, bring a pot of generously salted water to a boil. Add the pasta and cook until not quite al dente, about 5 minutes. Drain.

In a medium bowl, stir together the panko, melted butter, oregano, thyme, lemon zest, and ½ teaspoon salt.

When the squash is done, fish out and discard the sage, then use an immersion blender to puree the squash and milk to a smooth sauce. Stir in the cooked pasta, cheddar, Romano, and lots of pepper. Mix well, then transfer to an approximately 9 by 13-inch (23 by 33 cm) baking dish. Scatter the buttered crumbs across the top.

Bake until the mac 'n' squash is hot and bubbling and the crumb topping is crispy, about 20 minutes.

Do Ahead Up to 2 days ahead, follow the recipe through the step where you scatter the buttered crumbs, then cover the dish and refrigerate. About 30 minutes before you want to serve, remove the cover from the dish, and pop into the oven.

Butternut Raviolini with Fried Sage Butter Sauce

Serves 6

Shaping raviolini (little ravioli) by hand is a labor of love, for sure. Your guests will be delighted and will feel so loved. And this recipe is also a fun one to do as a group activity—try it for an interactive dinner party with friends who like to cook. You can make the fresh pasta dough, if you want, but usually you can find excellent prerolled fresh pasta sheets at Italian markets and well-stocked grocery stores. They'll save you time, and you're already doing quite a lot filling and shaping each raviolino, so why not take the shortcut?

SAUCE

½ cup (120 ml) extra-virgin olive oil

1 small bunch fresh sage, leaves picked

1 stick (4 ounces/115 g) unsalted butter

¼ teaspoon fine sea salt

FILLING

Fine sea salt

1 medium butternut squash (about 2 pounds/910 g), peeled and cut into ¾-inch (2 cm) cubes

1 large egg

½ cup (50 g) freshly grated Parmigiano-Reggiano cheese, plus more for serving

Freshly ground black pepper

FOR ASSEMBLY

Semolina flour, for dusting

1 pound (450 g) fresh pasta sheets

Fine sea salt

Make the sauce: Line a plate with paper towels. In a small saucepan, warm the olive oil over medium-high heat for 2 minutes. Add a sage leaf and see if it sizzles immediately. If it does, add the rest of the sage leaves and cook, stirring or swirling a few times, until the bubbling subsides and the sage turns a more vibrant shade of green, about 20 seconds. Use a slotted spoon to transfer the fried sage to the paper towels and let the oil cool to room temperature. (The sage oil will be used when making the filling.)

In a large skillet, melt the butter over medium-high heat. Add the salt and cook, stirring or swirling occasionally, until the butter browns, 4 to 6 minutes. Remove the pan from the heat. Now your sauce is ready to go and you can focus on shaping the pasta.

Prepare the filling: Bring a large pot of salted water to a boil. Add the squash cubes and cook until tender when poked with a fork, 15 to 20 minutes. Drain.

Transfer the cooked squash to a large bowl and use a fork or a potato masher to mash it to a chunky puree. Mix in the egg, Parmigiano, ¼ cup (60 ml) of the reserved sage oil, ½ teaspoon salt, and lots of pepper. Use the filling right away or refrigerate until you're ready to shape the pasta.

To assemble: Lightly dust a sheet pan with semolina.

Lay one sheet of fresh pasta on a clean work surface. Spoon heaped teaspoons of the butternut filling along one long edge of the pasta sheet, about ¾ inch (2 cm) in from the edge, spacing them 1 inch (2.5 cm) apart from one another. Brush the area around each mound of filling with water, then fold the pasta sheet lengthwise over the filling and press gently to seal and squeeze out the air. Use a fluted pasta cutter to cut along the top of the row and then in between the mounds to create individual little ravioli (raviolini). Place them on the prepared sheet pan. Repeat with the remaining pasta sheets and filling.

When ready to serve, bring a large pot of generously salted water to a boil. Return the pan of browned butter to medium heat and use your fingers to crumble in the fried sage.

Add the raviolini to the boiling water and cook until just barely tender, about 2 minutes. Use a slotted spoon to transfer them directly to the pan of browned butter. Stir in ½ cup (120 ml) of the pasta cooking water. Increase the heat to medium-high and cook, shaking the pan gently, until the sauce thickens slightly and coats the pasta, 2 to 3 minutes.

Serve hot, showering each plate with Parmigiano.

Pasta Carbonara

Serves 6

For a truly special party (and one that's small enough that you can pull this off successfully), make a dish that's cooked à la minute—something that necessitates careful attention and tastes best served right away. Pasta carbonara fits the bill.

Fine sea salt

3 large eggs

3 large egg yolks

½ cup (50 g) freshly grated Parmigiano-Reggiano cheese

½ cup (50 g) freshly grated Pecorino Romano cheese

Freshly ground black pepper

2 tablespoons extra-virgin olive oil

4 ounces (115 g) guanciale, pancetta, or bacon, cut into ¼-inch (6 mm) pieces

1½ pounds (680 g) spaghetti

Bring a large pot of salted water to a boil.

Find a bowl large enough that it'll rest over the pot without its bottom touching the bottom of the pot. Fill the bowl with hot water from the tap and set the bowl aside.

In a medium bowl, whisk together the whole eggs, egg yolks, Parmigiano, Romano, ¼ teaspoon salt, and as much black pepper as you can grind until your arm hurts.

In a large skillet, warm the olive oil over medium heat. Add the guanciale and cook, stirring occasionally, until the fat renders and the pork crisps a little but doesn't get too hard. Remove the pan from the heat.

Add the spaghetti to the boiling water and cook until just shy of al dente. Reserving 1 cup (240 ml) of the cooking water, drain the pasta and transfer directly to the skillet with the guanciale. Cook, stirring constantly, over medium-low heat for 1 minute.

Pour the water from the large bowl into the pot used for boiling the pasta and bring to a simmer. Transfer the pasta and guanciale to the empty large bowl, add the egg/cheese mixture and about ¼ cup (60 ml) of the reserved cooking water, and stir vigorously to coat the pasta in the sauce. Set the bowl over the pot of simmering water and keep stirring while the pasta and sauce cook gently, about 5 minutes. If the sauce looks very thick, add another splash of the reserved cooking water. When the sauce is creamy, has thickened slightly, and clings heavily to the noodles, the pasta carbonara is ready to serve.

Creating Your Own Menu

Creating a custom menu for a party can feel a little intimidating. You might be asking yourself: How do I know which dishes go together flavorwise? Are people going to like the food? Where do I even start? Don't worry, the process of putting together a menu is simple and meant to be fun. This book offers an entire chapter of sample menus that you can follow exactly (see page 270), but they also act as good inspiration for planning your own menu. Modify them however you like or follow these steps to create your own menu:

1 **Start with a theme.** A theme doesn't have to be silly or corny! The theme can be as simple as the reason for the party. Are you gathering with friends on a Sunday night? Is it a holiday? Think about the purpose of the party, the vibe you're going for. There are no wrong answers here. For cozy vibes, start by considering a roast as part of the menu. For casual parties, the food should match in terms of ease. If you're celebrating something, maybe there's a festive drink you want to serve that can act as the starting point for menu planning. Someone's birthday? What's their favorite? Try planning your menu around that.

2 **Cook food you want to eat.** Try not to worry too much about what your guests will like. Instead, start with your own cravings. What sounds good to you? Have you been wanting to eat Pasta Carbonara (page 191) ever since you watched that travel show on Italy? You will have a way better time cooking if the food is something you really want to eat. If you're a vegetarian, cook a vegetarian meal and do not—under any circumstances—feel like you need to apologize to your guests. In fact, never apologize for food you've cooked.

3 **Fill in the gaps.** Once you've got your theme figured out and you know at least one dish that you want to cook and eat, it's time to build out from there. Is there another dish that would taste great alongside the first one? Think about complementary flavors and textures: Bread is nice for dipping into soup or mopping up the flavorful juices of a roasted chicken (see Roasted Chickens and Schmaltzy-Oven Potatoes, page 159); spicy foods pair well with cooling sides like yogurt-based sauces or chilled salads; a meaty dish like Bavette with Chimichurri (page 153) calls for a starchy companion.

NAVIGATING DIETARY RESTRICTIONS

As a host, your primary job is to make your guests feel comfortable, cared for, and well fed. That means accommodating any dietary restrictions. When you're inviting someone over for a party, ask them if there are any foods they don't eat. You can plan your menu accordingly. For example, let's say you'd like to serve Minty Pea Soup with Crème Fraîche Swirl (page 89) but need it to be vegetarian. Simply swap the chicken broth for vegetable stock, and leave out the grated Parmigiano-Reggiano if your vegetarian guests don't eat it. (Some cheeses, including Pecorino Romano, Gruyère, and Manchego, are traditionally made with rennet, a nonvegetarian ingredient.) If any of your guests are vegan, you don't need to cook an entirely vegan menu; just make sure there are a few dishes they can eat that will leave them feeling satiated. Remember to think about each part of the meal, too. Gluten-free guests will especially appreciate a dessert they can enjoy. Gluten has a habit of sneaking

into ingredients you might not expect, such as soy sauce (use tamari instead!) and a lot of packaged goods. But these days there's a wide variety of fantastic products intended for eaters of all kinds. Gluten-free crackers are delicious, vegan yogurt is made from cashews, and options for nondairy milk are seemingly endless. In accommodating your guests' dietary restrictions, you might even discover a new-to-you food that becomes an all-time favorite.

VISUALIZE SUCCESS

Visualizing conditions our brain for success. This studied technique of imagining yourself hitting a home run or kicking a goal is actually something elite athletes use to perform successfully when it's game time. Of course, hosting a party is not the same as playing a sport, and there's no need to get too competitive, but it can be greatly helpful to do an imaginary walk-through or dress rehearsal of the party. When you picture how—and in what order—you are going to cook each dish, you might realize that the cake can't bake while you're roasting the chicken, either because the two dishes won't fit together in the oven or because the recipes require different oven temperatures. Mental planning is valuable and free, and it takes no more effort than lying down on your couch and closing your eyes, which also happens to be relaxing! Relaxing before a party is definitely important, too.

Desserts

Julia Child once said, "A party without cake is just a meeting." She was certainly right about festive gatherings needing something sweet, but there are many options for dessert. Tarts like Cranberry Meringue Tart (page 207) and Barley and Salted Caramel Pine Nut Tart (page 211) are unexpected but beautiful options. So, too, is Giant Pavlova with Chamomile Cream and Citrus (page 213), which feels especially celebratory given its jumbo size. And cookies of all kinds make for ideal last bites at a standing-room-only party.

Pistachio Butter Cake with Apricot and Candied Rose Petals

Makes one 8-inch (20 cm) cake

The batter for this cake starts by making fresh pistachio butter, which is just grinding pistachios in a food processor until creamy. The richness of pistachio butter adds pleasing heft to the cake layers, giving them a texture like pound cake. A layer of apricot jam in the middle adds fruity sweetness, and a flurry of candied rose petals on top creates a truly gorgeous and romantic finale. You can use any kind of edible flower you like for the candied petals, but be sure to seek out an organic bouquet that hasn't been sprayed with any pesticides.

CANDIED ROSE PETALS

12 organic roses, preferably in a variety of colors

1 or 2 egg whites

Pinch of fine sea salt, plus more as needed

Granulated sugar

CAKE

Softened butter, for the pans

1⅔ cups (210 g) all-purpose flour

2½ teaspoons baking powder

½ teaspoon fine sea salt

1 cup (135 g) salted roasted pistachios

2 ounces (55 g) white chocolate, finely chopped

1 teaspoon pure vanilla extract

1 cup (200 g) plus 1 tablespoon granulated sugar

2 sticks (8 ounces/225 g) unsalted butter, at cool room temperature

3 large eggs

½ cup (125 g) plain whole-milk yogurt

FROSTING

1½ sticks (6 ounces/170 g) unsalted butter, at cool room temperature

2 cups (245 g) powdered sugar

Pinch of fine sea salt

1 or 2 lemons

FOR ASSEMBLY

1 (12-ounce/340 g) jar apricot jam

The night before you want to serve the cake, make the candied rose petals: Gently pluck the individual petals from the roses and pat them thoroughly dry. (The innermost petals are often too curled and tiny for candying—save them for your next bath!)

In a small bowl, whisk together 1 egg white and the salt until foamy. Working with 1 rose petal at a time, use a soft-bristled brush to paint both sides of the petal with egg white. Sprinkle a thin layer of granulated sugar evenly over both sides of the petal. Place the petal on a wire rack and repeat with the remaining petals, spacing them out on the rack so they don't overlap. (If you run out of egg white, just add a second egg white to the bowl and whisk in another pinch of salt.) Let the candied petals dry at room temperature overnight, or until crisp.

Make the cake: Preheat the oven to 350°F (180°C). Butter the sides of two 8-inch (21 cm) round cake pans and line the bottoms with rounds of parchment paper.

In a medium bowl, whisk together the flour, baking powder, and salt.

In a food processor, combine the pistachios, white chocolate, vanilla, and 1 tablespoon of the granulated sugar and blend until creamy and smooth, about 10 minutes.

In a stand mixer fitted with the paddle, beat the butter and remaining 1 cup (200 g) granulated sugar on medium-high speed until light and fluffy, about 4 minutes. Mix in the pistachio butter. Add the eggs one at a time, beating well after each addition. Mix in the yogurt. Finally, add the flour mixture and beat on low speed until just combined. Divide the batter evenly between the prepared pans.

Bake until golden brown and a toothpick inserted into the center comes out clean, about 30 minutes. If the cake layers are browning too quickly, cover them with foil and continue baking.

Let the cake layers cool for a few minutes in the pans, then invert them onto a wire rack, remove the parchment paper, and let cool completely.

Make the frosting: In a stand mixer fitted with the paddle, beat the butter, powdered sugar, salt, and finely grated zest of 1 lemon on medium-high speed until combined, 1 minute. While mixing, drizzle in the juice of 1 lemon. Beat until light, fluffy, and smooth, about 5 minutes. If the frosting is too thick, continue adding more lemon juice slowly, 1 teaspoon at a time, until the frosting is spreadable.

Place one cooled cake layer on a cake stand or serving plate. Spread the jam on top of the cake. Top with the second cake layer. Frost the top and sides of the cake with the lemon buttercream, smoothing it evenly and creating casual swoops on top. Decorate the cake with the candied rose petals. Slice and serve.

Cover any leftover cake slices with a glass cake stand dome (or loosely tent with plastic wrap) and store at room temperature. It'll taste best the day it's made, but one of my all-time favorite after-party treats is cake for breakfast with coffee.

DMW (Dark-Milk-White) Chocolate Layer Cake

Makes one 9-inch (23 cm) cake

Three layers—each flavored with a different kind of chocolate—make up this towering cake. But don't worry; you won't make three batters, just one that you divide into three different portions. Half the fun in making this dessert is decorating it with frosting. The instructions below, which make a gradient or ombré effect, are just one idea for how you might go about using the three different colors of frosting. Try tapping into your inner food stylist and coming up with your own way.

CAKE

Softened butter, for the pans

3 cups (375 g) all-purpose flour

2¼ teaspoons baking powder

¾ teaspoon baking soda

¾ teaspoon fine sea salt

3 sticks (12 ounces/340 g) unsalted butter, at cool room temperature

1¾ cups (350 g) granulated sugar

4 large eggs, at cool room temperature

1 tablespoon pure vanilla extract

1½ cups (360 ml) buttermilk

2 ounces (55 g) white chocolate, melted and cooled slightly

2 ounces (55 g) milk chocolate, melted and cooled slightly

⅓ cup (25 g) plus 3 tablespoons unsweetened cocoa powder

2 ounces (55 g) dark chocolate, melted and cooled slightly

2 tablespoons cocoa noir powder

FROSTING

4 sticks (16 ounces/455 g) unsalted butter, at cool room temperature

5 cups (625 g) powdered sugar, sifted

1 teaspoon fine sea salt

3 ounces (85 g) white chocolate, melted and cooled slightly

3 ounces (85 g) milk chocolate, melted and cooled slightly

3 ounces (85 g) dark chocolate, melted and cooled slightly

1 tablespoon cocoa noir powder

Buttermilk, as needed

Make the cake: Preheat the oven to 350°F (180°C). Butter the sides of three 9-inch (23 cm) round cake pans and line the bottoms with rounds of parchment paper. (If you have only two pans, bake two of the layers and then wash one pan and use it to bake the third layer.)

In a medium bowl, stir together the flour, baking powder, baking soda, and salt.

In a stand mixer fitted with the paddle, beat the butter and granulated sugar on medium-high speed until light and fluffy, about 4 minutes. ⟶

Scrape down the sides of the bowl with a rubber spatula. With the mixer running, add the eggs one at a time, beating well after each addition. Add the vanilla and mix well. Add half the flour mixture and half the buttermilk to the bowl and mix on low speed until incorporated. Add the remaining flour mixture and buttermilk and mix just until there are no visible streaks of flour. Divide the batter evenly among three bowls.

To the first bowl, mix in the white chocolate. To the second bowl, mix in the milk chocolate and ⅓ cup (25 g) of the unsweetened cocoa powder. To the third bowl, mix in the dark chocolate, cocoa noir powder, and remaining 3 tablespoons unsweetened cocoa powder. Scrape the batter from each bowl into one of the prepared cake pans, spreading it evenly and smoothing the tops with a clean rubber spatula (be careful not to mix the colors!).

Bake until the tops of the cakes bounce back when lightly pressed and a toothpick inserted into the centers comes out clean, 25 to 30 minutes.

Let the cakes cool in their pans for 5 minutes, then invert the pans onto a wire rack, lift the pans off the cakes, peel away the parchment paper, set the cake layers right side up, and let them cool to room temperature.

Make the frosting: In a stand mixer fitted with the paddle, combine the butter, powdered sugar, and salt. Beat on high speed until light and fluffy, about 5 minutes. Divide the frosting among three medium or large bowls, putting about equal amounts in two of the bowls and a little less in the third bowl. Stir the white chocolate into one bowl, the milk chocolate into the second bowl, and the dark chocolate and cocoa noir powder into the third bowl that has the smaller amount of frosting. If the frosting made with cocoa noir is too thick to spread easily, stir in a splash of buttermilk, 1 tablespoon at a time, until it's spreadable.

To assemble the cake, place the white chocolate layer on a serving plate. Frost it on the sides and top with the white chocolate frosting, leaving about ½ cup (60 g) of frosting in the bowl. Place the milk chocolate cake layer on top and frost it on the sides and top with the milk chocolate frosting, leaving about ½ cup (60 g) frosting in the bowl. Top with the dark chocolate cake layer and frost it on only the sides with the dark chocolate frosting, leaving about ½ cup (60 g) of frosting in the bowl. For the top of the cake, spread thick wavy stripes of the three different frostings. Serve the cake at room temperature and store any leftovers, loosely covered, in the refrigerator.

Upside-Down Blood Orange Semolina Cake

Makes one 9-inch (23 cm) cake

If you were on vacation in Sicily, this is the cake you'd eat in the afternoon, maybe with an espresso alongside. A slice for breakfast, perhaps? No judgment here, it's hard to turn down a slice of this dazzling cake, crowned with juicy baked blood orange slices. Transport your guests to the land of ocean breezes and Mediterranean sun by serving this cake at your next winter party. The sweet-tart orange syrup that gets drizzled over the baked cake helps it stay moist; it keeps well, tightly wrapped, at room temperature for a few days.

Softened butter, for the pan

5 blood oranges

2 cups (200 g) almond flour

1 cup (165 g) fine semolina flour

1½ teaspoons baking powder

¼ teaspoon fine sea salt

2 sticks (8 ounces/225 g) unsalted butter, at room temperature

2 cups (400 g) sugar

4 large eggs

1 teaspoon orange blossom water

Preheat the oven to 350°F (180°C). Line the bottom of a 9-inch (23 cm) round cake pan with a round of parchment paper and generously butter the sides.

Using a sharp knife, cut off the top and bottom of 3 of the blood oranges. Working with one blood orange at a time, stand the fruit on a cutting board on one cut side so it doesn't roll around. Place the blade of a knife at the top of the blood orange and cut down, tracing the curved line of the fruit, to remove a section of the peel, white pith, and the membrane, exposing the fruit. Rotate the blood orange and continue cutting away the peel and pith until you've removed it all. Go back and trim any membrane or pith still clinging to the fruit. Slice the blood oranges crosswise into wheels ¼ inch (6 mm) thick. Arrange them in a single layer, overlapping slightly if needed to fit, in the prepared pan.

Finely grate the zest from the remaining 2 blood oranges and squeeze the juice. Set both the zest and juice aside.

In a large bowl, combine the almond flour, semolina, baking powder, and salt.

In a stand mixer fitted with the paddle, beat the butter and 1½ cups (300 g) of the sugar on medium-high speed until lightened in color and fluffy, about 5 minutes. Add the eggs one at a time, beating well after each addition. Mix in the orange blossom water and blood orange zest. Add the flour mixture and mix on low speed until just incorporated. Scrape the batter into the prepared pan and gently smooth the surface without disturbing the fruit layer below.

Bake until the cake springs back when lightly pressed and a toothpick inserted into the center comes out clean, about 1 hour.

When the cake is almost done baking, in a small saucepan, combine ½ cup (120 ml) of the blood orange juice and the remaining ½ cup (100 g) sugar. Set over medium heat, stirring to dissolve the sugar. As soon as the mixture comes to a boil, remove the pan from the heat.

When the cake is done, let it cool in the pan for about 10 minutes, then poke a few holes in the cake with a toothpick and spoon the warm orange syrup over the top. Let the cake cool completely before inverting it onto a platter, slicing, and serving.

Cover any leftovers and store at room temperature for up to 3 days.

Candied Ginger Cupcakes

Makes 12 cupcakes

These look like classic yellow cupcakes, but they're flavored with warm, bright ginger. Cupcakes always make any gathering feel like a party. And if you happen to be transporting them, here's a trick: Once you've frosted them, place them back in the metal pan you baked them in, and you're ready to go! No need to bother with covering them, since you don't want to risk messing up the frosting. These are a sweet ending to the Pack-and-Go Picnic! menu (page 281) or any outdoor party. Cake flour in the batter helps keep the cupcakes extra soft and tender, although you can substitute all-purpose flour if that's what you've got.

CUPCAKES

1½ cups (180 g) cake flour

½ cup (85 g) candied ginger, finely chopped

2 teaspoons ground ginger

2 teaspoons baking powder

½ teaspoon fine sea salt

1 stick (4 ounces/115 g) unsalted butter, at cool room temperature

1 cup (200 g) granulated sugar

1 teaspoon pure vanilla extract

2 large eggs

½ cup (120 ml) whole milk

FROSTING

1 stick (4 ounces/115 g) unsalted butter, at cool room temperature

1½ cups (190 g) powdered sugar

Pinch of fine sea salt

Finely grated zest of 1 lemon

2 to 3 tablespoons heavy cream

TOPPING

24 thin strips of sliced candied ginger

Make the cupcakes: Preheat the oven to 350°F (180°C). Line 12 cups of a muffin tin with paper liners.

In a bowl, whisk together the flour, candied ginger, ground ginger, baking powder, and salt.

In a stand mixer fitted with the paddle, beat the butter, granulated sugar, and vanilla on medium-high speed until light and fluffy, 3 to 5 minutes. Add the eggs one at a time, beating well after each addition. Add one-third of the flour mixture and half of the milk. Mix on low speed to combine, then add another one-third of the flour mixture and the remaining milk. Mix on low speed just for a few seconds. Finally, add the last of the flour mixture and mix until just barely incorporated. Divide the batter evenly among the muffin cups, filling each about three-quarters full. →

Bake until springy when pressed lightly and a toothpick inserted into the center comes out clean, about 18 minutes.

Let the cupcakes cool in the pan for a few minutes before transferring them to a wire rack to cool completely.

Make the frosting: In a stand mixer fitted with the paddle, beat the butter on medium-high speed until fluffy, 3 to 5 minutes. With the mixer still on, gradually add the powdered sugar and continue beating until incorporated. Add the salt, lemon zest, and 2 tablespoons of the cream and mix on medium speed for 1 minute. If you'd like the frosting to be a bit looser, mix in another 1 tablespoon of cream.

Frost the top of the cooled cupcakes and garnish each one with 2 strips of candied ginger.

Do Ahead These taste best the day they're baked, but you can make the frosting ahead and store it in an airtight container in the refrigerator for up to 3 days. Let it warm up to room temperature before spreading on the cupcakes.

Cranberry Meringue Tart

Makes one 9-inch (23 cm) tart

It's as if traditional lemon meringue pie got a makeover and emerged pretty in pink and with a new set of fancy pants. The meringue topping hides the stunning cranberry-dyed filling, so it feels almost like a magic trick when you cut into the tart to reveal its fuchsia center. Try bringing this dessert to your family's next Thanksgiving dinner.

CRUST

¾ cup (75 g) almond flour

¾ cup (95 g) all-purpose flour, plus more for rolling

2 tablespoons sugar

½ teaspoon fine sea salt

1 stick (4 ounces/115 g) unsalted butter, sliced and chilled

3 to 4 tablespoons ice-cold water

CRANBERRY FILLING

12 ounces (340 g) fresh cranberries

1 cup (200 g) sugar

½ cup (120 ml) fresh lemon juice (from 3 or 4 small lemons)

¼ teaspoon fine sea salt

1 stick (4 ounces/115 g) unsalted butter, at room temperature, cut into 8 pieces

2 large eggs

2 large egg yolks (save the whites for the meringue)

MERINGUE

4 large egg whites

¼ teaspoon cream of tartar

¼ teaspoon fine sea salt

½ cup (100 g) sugar

1 teaspoon pure vanilla extract

Make the crust: In a large bowl, stir together the almond flour, all-purpose flour, sugar, and salt. Using your fingertips, rub the butter into the flour mixture until the butter pieces are the size of corn kernels. Pour in 3 tablespoons of the ice-cold water and quickly but gently knead into a shaggy ball of dough. If the dough is too dry and won't come together, add another 1 tablespoon water and try again. Wrap the dough in plastic, making sure to include any crumbs of flour from the bottom of the bowl, and refrigerate for at least 1 hour or up to 3 days.

On a lightly floured surface, roll out the dough to an 11-inch (28 cm) round. Place the dough in a 9-inch (23 cm) fluted tart pan with a removable bottom, gently pressing it into the sides and corners and trimming any excess dough that hangs over the edge of the pan. Use a fork to prick the dough in several places. Freeze for 20 minutes.

Meanwhile, preheat the oven to 350°F (180°C). →

Bake the crust until lightly golden, about 20 minutes. Remove the crust and let it cool slightly. Keep the oven on.

While the crust bakes, make the cranberry filling: In a medium saucepan, combine the cranberries, sugar, lemon juice, and salt. Cook over medium heat, stirring occasionally, until the cranberries have all burst and their juices have thickened slightly, about 10 minutes. Transfer to a high-powered blender and puree until smooth. Strain through a fine-mesh sieve into a medium bowl. Add the butter and stir until melted.

Rinse out the saucepan, add the whole eggs and egg yolks to it, and whisk to blend. While whisking constantly, slowly pour about ½ cup (120 ml) of the cranberry mixture into the pan, then add the rest of the cranberry mixture and set the pan over low heat. Cook, stirring often with a silicone spatula, until thickened, about 10 minutes.

Pour the cranberry filling into the prebaked crust and smooth the surface. Bake until the filling is wiggly but set, 10 to 15 minutes. Remove the tart and switch the oven to broil.

Meanwhile, make the meringue: In a small saucepan that the stand mixer bowl can sit over, bring 1 inch (2.5 cm) of water to a boil.

In the stand mixer fitted with the whisk, combine the egg whites, cream of tartar, and salt. Whisk on medium-high speed until foamy, about 1 minute. Gradually add the sugar, one large spoonful at a time, beating well after each addition. Transfer the bowl to rest over the simmering water, making sure the bottom of the bowl doesn't touch the water. Cook, whisking constantly, until the sugar dissolves and the mixture feels hotter than body temperature when you touch it with your finger. Return the bowl to the stand mixer and whisk on medium-high speed until the meringue holds soft peaks, about 5 minutes. Mix in the vanilla.

Spread the meringue in dramatic swoops over the cranberry filling, spreading it all the way to the edges to completely cover the filling. Place the tart under the broiler and cook until the meringue is nicely browned in a few places, 2 to 3 minutes. (Keep a watchful eye on the meringue as it broils.)

Let cool for at least 1 hour before cutting into slices and serving. This tart is best eaten the day it's made but can be loosely covered and refrigerated for up to 3 days.

Barley and Salted Caramel Pine Nut Tart

Makes one 9-inch (23 cm) tart

Malted barley syrup, which is used in the filling here, is about half as sweet as white sugar and has a slow, drippy texture like that of molasses. To echo the toasted grain flavor of the syrup, there's barley flour in the crust for this tart. Bob's Red Mill has a great barley flour, and you can also usually find it in natural foods stores.

CRUST

¾ cup (85 g) barley flour

¾ cup (95 g) all-purpose flour, plus more for rolling

2 tablespoons sugar

½ teaspoon fine sea salt

1 stick (4 ounces/115 g) unsalted butter, sliced and chilled

3 to 4 tablespoons ice-cold water

FILLING

1½ cups (205 g) pine nuts

¾ cup (150 g) sugar

3 tablespoons room-temperature water

⅓ cup (80 ml) heavy cream

2 tablespoons extra-virgin olive oil

2 tablespoons unsalted butter, cut into 6 pieces

1 tablespoon malted barley syrup

1 tablespoon honey

1 teaspoon pure vanilla extract

1 teaspoon flaky sea salt

Make the crust: In a large bowl, stir together the barley flour, all-purpose flour, sugar, and fine salt. Using your fingertips, rub the butter into the flour mixture until the butter pieces are the size of corn kernels. Pour in 3 tablespoons of the ice-cold water and quickly but gently knead into a shaggy ball of dough. If the dough is too dry and won't come together, add another 1 tablespoon water and try again. Shape the dough into a disk, place in the bowl, cover with the butter stick wrapper, and refrigerate for 1 hour. Or wrap more tightly and refrigerate for up to 3 days.

On a lightly floured surface, roll out the dough to an 11-inch (28 cm) round. Place the dough in a 9-inch (23 cm) fluted tart pan with a removable bottom, gently pressing it into the sides and corners and trimming any excess dough that hangs over the edge of the pan. Use a fork to prick the dough in several places. Freeze for 15 minutes.

Meanwhile, preheat the oven to 350°F (180°C). ⟶

Bake the crust until lightly golden, about 20 minutes.

Make the filling: While the crust is in the oven, spread the pine nuts on a sheet pan and toast them, stirring once or twice, until golden brown, 5 to 8 minutes. Remove the crust and nuts and let them cool, but leave the oven on and increase the temperature to 400°F (200°C).

In a medium saucepan, combine the sugar and water. Cook over medium heat, stirring until the sugar dissolves. Stop stirring and continue cooking, swirling the pan every so often, until the caramel is amber, about 10 minutes. Remove the pan from the heat and carefully pour in the cream—it will bubble! Stir until smooth, then mix in the olive oil, butter, malted barley syrup, honey, vanilla, flaky salt, and toasted pine nuts.

Pour the filling mixture into the prebaked crust, return to the oven, and bake until the filling is bubbling and slightly darker golden brown, about 20 minutes.

Let cool to room temperature, then pop into the fridge for 1 hour to chill. Remove the tart from its pan and serve. Cover and store any leftover tart at room temperature for up to 2 days.

Giant Pavlova with Chamomile Cream and Citrus

Serves 8

This giant pavlova is ready to party and will be loved by eaters of all kinds—especially any of your friends avoiding gluten. The chamomile cream is unique and even a little intriguing. It's made by steeping loose chamomile tea in heavy cream and then whipping that cream until it holds soft, floppy peaks. You can't see the chamomile, but the floral, heady flavor shines through and makes people ask, "What's special about this whipped cream?"

CHAMOMILE CREAM

2 cups (480 ml) heavy cream

¼ cup (8 g) loose chamomile tea

1 tablespoon powdered sugar

MERINGUE

6 large egg whites

¼ teaspoon fine sea salt

1½ cups (300 g) granulated sugar

1 tablespoon cornstarch, sifted

1½ teaspoons white wine vinegar

1 teaspoon pure vanilla extract

TOPPING

1 large pink grapefruit

2 Cara Cara or navel oranges

1 Meyer lemon or blood orange

Fresh chamomile blossoms, lemon blossoms, or rosemary blossoms, for garnish

Make the chamomile cream: In a small saucepan, combine the cream, loose chamomile tea, and powdered sugar. Warm gently over medium-low heat until the cream starts steaming and tiny bubbles appear around the edges of the pan. Carefully watch the cream, and as soon as you see bubbles, pour the mixture into a container, cover, and refrigerate until completely chilled, at least 2 hours or up to 2 days.

Preheat the oven to 350°F (180°C).

Using a pencil, trace a 14-inch (35 cm) circle on a piece of parchment paper, then flip the paper over and place it on a large sheet pan. (If you have a round baking sheet like the kind used for pizza, it's perfect here.)

Make the meringue: In a stand mixer fitted with the whisk, combine the egg whites and salt. Beat on high speed for 1 minute. With the mixer running on high, gradually add the granulated sugar and beat until shiny, stiff peaks form, 2 to 3 minutes. Use a rubber spatula to gently fold in the cornstarch, vinegar, and vanilla. Transfer the mixture to the

prepared parchment, smoothing it out into a round disk and using the circle as a guide.

Place in the oven, immediately lower the oven temperature to 300°F (150°C), and bake until crisp on the outside but still soft inside, 1 hour 15 minutes.

Turn off the oven and leave the meringue inside with the door closed until completely cool.

For the topping, suprême the citrus: Using a sharp knife, cut off the top and bottom of the grapefruit. Stand the fruit on a cutting board on one cut side so it doesn't roll around. Place the blade of a knife at the top of the grapefruit and cut down, tracing the curved line of the fruit, to remove a section of the peel, white pith, and membrane to expose the fruit. Rotate the grapefruit and continue cutting away the peel and pith until you've removed it all. Go back and trim any pith or membrane still clinging to the fruit. Holding the grapefruit in your nondominant hand, cut along each thin white membrane to release the segments of fruit. Repeat to suprême the Cara Cara oranges and Meyer lemon, collecting all the citrus fruit segments in a bowl. Cover and refrigerate until ready to serve.

Just before serving, peel the parchment paper off the meringue and place it on a serving platter. Use the back of a wooden spoon to gently crack the meringue in a few places.

Remove the chamomile cream from the fridge and strain through a fine-mesh sieve into a mixer bowl. Whip until the cream holds soft peaks, then spread it across the meringue. Top with the citrus segments, garnish with fresh blossoms, and serve. Pavlovas are best eaten immediately after you've topped them with whipped cream.

Do Ahead You can make the meringue ahead and, once it is cool, store it in an airtight container at room temperature for up to 2 days. The citrus suprêmes can be stored in an airtight container in the refrigerator for up to 2 days.

Strawberry Jam Thumbprint Cookies

Makes about 24 cookies

You'll want to create the thumbprint indentation in these cookies while they're still hot from the oven. In order to not burn yourself by using your actual thumb, use a wine cork! There's usually a loose one rolling around at a party.

1½ cups (205 g) pistachios

⅓ cup (75 g) demerara sugar

2 sticks (8 ounces/225 g) unsalted butter, at cool room temperature

½ cup (100 g) granulated sugar

2 large egg yolks

1 teaspoon pure vanilla extract

1½ cups (190 g) all-purpose flour

1 teaspoon baking powder

½ teaspoon fine sea salt

⅓ cup (105 g) strawberry jam

Position racks in the top and center of the oven and preheat the oven to 375°F (190°C). Line two sheet pans with parchment paper.

In a food processor, pulse the pistachios until they are finely ground. Measure out ¼ cup (25 g) of the ground pistachios and place in a bowl. Stir in the demerara sugar and set aside for rolling the cookies.

In a stand mixer fitted with the paddle, beat the butter and granulated sugar on medium-high speed until light and fluffy, about 3 minutes. Scrape down the sides of the bowl. Mix in the egg yolks and vanilla. Add the flour, baking powder, salt, and ground pistachios and mix on low speed until just combined.

Scoop 1-tablespoon portions of the cookie dough, roll in the demerara sugar mixture, and place on the prepared sheet pans, evenly spaced.

Bake for 6 minutes. Remove the sheets from the oven and use your thumb or a wine cork to create a shallow indent in the middle of each cookie. Try to give the cookie an even thickness on all sides. Return the sheets to the oven, switching racks and rotating the sheets front to back, and bake until golden brown, 6 to 8 minutes more.

Let the cookies cool for a few minutes on the sheet pans, then transfer to a wire rack. Fill each cookie with about ½ teaspoon jam.

Once completely cool, store in an airtight container at room temperature for up to 2 days.

Pignoli

Makes about 24 cookies

One surefire strategy for baking a spectacular gluten-free dessert is to look to the classic sweets that are gluten-free to begin with. These traditional Italian cookies studded with pine nuts are made from naturally gluten-free almond flour and almond paste. They're guaranteed to be enjoyed by both friends who don't eat gluten and those who do.

¾ cup (100 g) pine nuts

8 ounces (225 g) almond paste, crumbled

¾ cup (75 g) almond flour

½ cup (100 g) granulated sugar

½ cup (65 g) powdered sugar

½ teaspoon fine sea salt

1 large egg white

2 teaspoons pure vanilla extract

Position racks in the top and center of the oven and preheat the oven to 300°F (150°C). Line two sheet pans with parchment paper.

In a medium skillet, toast the pine nuts over medium heat, stirring and shaking the pan frequently, until golden brown, 2 to 3 minutes. Watch the pine nuts carefully, as they can quickly go from browned to burnt. Transfer the toasted pine nuts to a medium bowl.

In a food processor, combine the almond paste, almond flour, granulated sugar, powdered sugar, and salt. Pulse until the mixture looks like sand. Add the egg white and vanilla and pulse until a soft dough forms.

Scoop heaped 1-tablespoon portions of dough into the bowl of toasted pine nuts and roll gently to coat the dough balls. Place them on the prepared sheet pans, spacing them out as much as possible. (There should be 12 dough balls on each sheet.)

Bake until golden, 20 to 25 minutes, switching racks and rotating the sheets front to back about halfway through.

Let cool completely on the sheet pans. Once completely cool, store in an airtight container at room temperature for up to 2 days.

Pignoli *(bottom left)* and Halva Choc-Chip Shortbread *(top right)*

Halva Choc-Chip Shortbread

Makes about 24 cookies

These easy slice-and-bake cookies will fit right in at pretty much any party. (When is a chocolate chip cookie ever not a good idea?) Halva, the Persian confection usually made from sesame seeds, is a surprising but lovely addition to the cookie dough. You can find it online (see Sources, page 294) or in Middle Eastern grocery stores.

1½ sticks (6 ounces/170 g) unsalted butter, at room temperature

½ cup (100 g) granulated sugar

¼ cup packed (55 g) brown sugar

½ teaspoon fine sea salt

1 large egg yolk

1 teaspoon pure vanilla extract

2 cups (250 g) all-purpose flour

1 (3.5-ounce/100 g) bar dark chocolate, chopped to gravel-size pieces

3½ ounces (100 g) halva, broken into small pieces

In a stand mixer fitted with the paddle, beat the butter, granulated sugar, brown sugar, and salt on medium-high speed until light and fluffy, about 4 minutes. Mix in the egg yolk and vanilla. Add the flour and mix on low speed until just combined. Using a rubber spatula, gently fold in the chocolate and halva.

Place the dough on a large sheet of parchment paper. Fold the paper over the dough and use your hands to roll and shape the dough into a log about 15 inches (38 cm) long. Wrap with the parchment, twisting the ends like a Tootsie Roll to seal, and refrigerate until firm, at least 2 hours or up to 3 days.

Position racks in the top and center of the oven and preheat the oven to 350°F (180°C). Line two sheet pans with parchment paper.

Using a serrated knife, cut the log into slices ½ inch (1.3 cm) thick. Place them on the prepared sheet pans, spacing them as far apart as possible.

Bake until the cookie edges are golden, about 15 minutes, switching racks and rotating the sheets front to back about halfway through.

Let cool on the sheets for a few minutes, then transfer to a wire rack to cool completely. Once completely cool, store in an airtight container at room temperature for up to 2 days.

Marbled Matcha Snickerdoodles

Makes about 16 cookies

Snickerdoodle cookies get their characteristic snap and crinkle from cream of tartar in the dough. These cookies are marbled green with matcha and inspired by the wonderful cookies at Bossie's Kitchen in Santa Barbara, California. Matcha quality can vary greatly and the highest-quality stuff is pricey, but because you're going to be mixing this matcha into cookie dough and baking it in a hot oven, you can use a middle-grade matcha and it will work well. Save the best ceremonial-grade matcha for drinking!

1½ cups (190 g) all-purpose flour

1 teaspoon cream of tartar

½ teaspoon baking soda

¼ teaspoon fine sea salt

4 tablespoons (½ stick/55 g) unsalted butter, melted

¼ cup (50 g) vegetable shortening, melted

¾ cup packed (160 g) brown sugar

1 large egg

1 teaspoon pure vanilla extract

1½ tablespoons matcha

½ cup (100 g) granulated sugar, for rolling

In a medium bowl, stir together the flour, cream of tartar, baking soda, and salt.

In another bowl, combine the melted butter, shortening, and brown sugar. Whisk until fully combined. Add the egg and vanilla and whisk vigorously for 1 minute. Use a rubber spatula to gently fold in the flour mixture, without overmixing. Transfer half of the cookie dough to a sheet of parchment paper, spreading it out about 1 inch (2.5 cm) thick. Add the matcha to the dough remaining in the bowl and gently fold until incorporated. Scoop the matcha dough on top of the nonmatcha dough, spreading it to cover but not worrying about imperfections— they are what will make the marble beautiful. Use the rubber spatula to gather the dough into the middle, folding it in on itself to create a marble effect. Place the cookie dough in the refrigerator to chill for 20 minutes.

While the dough chills, position racks in the top and center of the oven and preheat the oven to 375°F (190°C). Line two sheet pans with parchment paper. ⟶

Place the granulated sugar in a small bowl. Use a 2-tablespoon cookie scoop or measuring spoons to scoop the marbled dough into balls. Drop the balls one at a time into the granulated sugar. Roll to coat on all sides, then place on the prepared sheet pans, evenly spaced.

Bake until the cookies are cracked and domed, 6 to 8 minutes, switching racks and rotating the sheets front to back about halfway through.

Let cool slightly on the sheet pan and serve warm.

Once completely cool, store the cookies in an airtight container at room temperature for up to 2 days. You can reheat on a sheet pan in a 200°F (90°C) oven for 5 minutes, if you'd like, but it's not necessary; the cookies will still taste great at room temperature.

Salted Almond Cantuccini

Makes about 24 cantuccini

Biscotti from Tuscany are usually called cantuccini and almost always have almonds in them. This version takes the importance of salt in desserts quite seriously and uses salted almonds plus a big pinch of salt in the dough. Don't worry, the cookies don't taste too salty—you'll hardly notice it; their sweetness is just nicely counterbalanced. There's a special technique for shaping cantuccini: You scoop the cookie dough onto the sheet pans and then use wet hands to smooth the dough into two long logs. Into the oven they go, and it is only after they have baked that you cut them into individual biscotti and put them back in the oven to crisp up a little further. Serve these alongside coffee at any time of day.

2 cups (250 g) all-purpose flour

2 teaspoons baking powder

½ teaspoon fine sea salt

1 stick (4 ounces/115 g) unsalted butter, at room temperature

¾ cup (150 g) sugar

2 large eggs

1 cup (140 g) salted roasted almonds

1 teaspoon pure almond extract

Preheat the oven to 350°F (180°C). Line a sheet pan with parchment paper.

In a small bowl, whisk together the flour, baking powder, and salt.

In a stand mixer fitted with the paddle, beat the butter and sugar on medium-high speed until light and fluffy, about 5 minutes. Use a rubber spatula to scrape down the sides of the bowl after about 2 minutes. Add the eggs one at a time, mixing well after each addition. Add the flour mixture and mix on low speed until almost fully incorporated, then add the almonds and almond extract and use a rubber spatula to fold them in.

Scoop the dough by the large spoonful onto the prepared sheet pan, creating two rough logs, each about 2 inches (5 cm) across. Wet your hands and use them to smooth the surface of the logs.

Bake until golden brown and slightly firm, 25 to 30 minutes.

Let the logs cool on the pan for 30 minutes. Transfer the logs to a cutting board. Use a serrated knife to cut the logs on a diagonal into slices ½ inch (1.3 cm) thick. Place the slices, cut sides down, on the sheet pan. (They don't need to be spaced out at all.)

Return to the oven and bake for 10 minutes. Flip and continue baking until golden and crisp, 5 to 10 minutes more.

Do Ahead Cantuccini keep very well stored in an airtight container like a big cookie jar. They'll still be crisp after several days, even up to 1 week. Just make sure they are completely cool before storing them.

3 WAYS TO TRANSFORM STORE-BOUGHT DESSERTS

1   Turn your home into an ice cream parlor by serving a few different pints of store-bought ice cream with all the toppings: warm chocolate sauce, caramel sauce, rainbow sprinkles, Maraschino or Amarena cherries, whipped cream, crushed Oreos, gummy bears, and so on.

2   Scatter store-bought meringue cookies on a platter, dollop with freshly whipped cream, and top with fresh berries. They're like personal mini pavlovas!

3   Make parfaits by layering a dollop of freshly whipped cream, a spoonful of store-bought lemon curd, and a handful of crumbled store-bought ginger cookies in small, pretty glasses. Serve with long-handled spoons, if you have them.

Ube Amaretti Cookies

Makes about 24 cookies

Amaretti cookies are classically made from three simple ingredients: ground almonds, egg whites, and sugar. They bake up to be crisp on the outside and satisfyingly chewy on the inside, but in this version they are also vibrantly purple and taste like sweet, vanilla-scented ube. Look for freeze-dried blueberries at Trader Joe's or natural foods stores. Ube extract is easy to buy online. For an Italian cookie party, you could serve these alongside the Pignoli (page 219) and Blackberry Mottled Occhi di Bue (page 228).

¼ cup (6.5 g) freeze-dried blueberries

½ cup (60 g) powdered sugar

2 large egg whites

¼ teaspoon cream of tartar

2 cups (200 g) almond flour

¾ cup (150 g) granulated sugar

¼ teaspoon baking powder

¼ teaspoon fine sea salt

1 teaspoon ube extract

Position racks in the top and center of the oven and preheat the oven to 300°F (150°C). Line two sheet pans with parchment paper.

In a food processor, process the freeze-dried blueberries to a fine powder. Add the powdered sugar and pulse to combine, then transfer the blueberry-sugar mixture to a shallow bowl.

In a stand mixer fitted with the whisk (or in a large bowl, using an electric mixer), whip the egg whites and cream of tartar until soft peaks form. Add the almond flour, granulated sugar, baking powder, salt, and ube extract. Use a rubber spatula to fold everything together until the batter is homogeneous and has the texture of paste.

Scoop up 1-tablespoon balls and roll them in the blueberry-sugar mixture until thoroughly coated. Place them on the prepared sheet pans, spaced evenly apart, and gently press each one with your palm to slightly flatten.

Bake the cookies until they're just barely cooked through and light golden brown on the bottoms, about 20 minutes, switching racks and rotating the sheets front to back about halfway through.

Transfer to a wire rack to cool completely. Once completely cool, store in an airtight container at room temperature for up to 2 days.

Blackberry Mottled Occhi di Bue

Makes about 24 sandwich cookies

In Italian, *occhi di bue* means "bull's eyes," a reference to the look of these jam-filled sandwich cookies. You'll usually find the same combination of plain cookies and red fruit jam in pasticcerie around Italy. This recipe is a completely nontraditional version that has streaks of midnight dark cocoa noir in the cookie dough and correspondingly inky blackberry jam in the center, which makes them a little richer and a little fruitier. When it's your turn to be a guest at someone else's party, these cookies would be a sweet gift to bring for the host.

3 cups (375 g) all-purpose flour, plus more for rolling

1 cup (100 g) almond flour

1 teaspoon baking powder

½ teaspoon fine sea salt

1 tablespoon cocoa noir

3 sticks (12 ounces/340 g) unsalted butter, at room temperature

1½ cups (300 g) granulated sugar

2 large eggs

1½ cups (480 g) blackberry jam

Powdered sugar

In a large bowl, stir together 1½ cups (190 g) of the all-purpose flour, ½ cup (50 g) of the almond flour, ½ teaspoon of the baking powder, and ¼ teaspoon of the salt.

In a medium bowl, stir together the cocoa noir and the remaining 1½ cups (190 g) all-purpose flour, ½ cup (50 g) almond flour, ½ teaspoon baking powder, and ¼ teaspoon salt.

In a stand mixer fitted with the paddle, beat the butter and sugar on medium-high speed until fluffy and lightened in color, about 5 minutes. Add the eggs one at a time, mixing well after each addition. Scoop half of the mixture out of the mixer into the large bowl with the plain flour mixture and stir until just incorporated.

Add the cocoa/flour mixture from the medium bowl into the stand mixer bowl and beat on low speed until just incorporated.

On a floured surface, divide each of the doughs into 6 equal pieces and arrange them in alternating colors like a checkerboard on a piece of parchment paper. Smash the pieces together and knead briefly, only once or twice, to marble the two colors together.

Divide the dough evenly in half, pat each one into a disk that's about 1 inch (2.5 cm) thick, and wrap tightly in plastic. Refrigerate for at least 2 hours.

Position racks in the top and center of the oven and preheat the oven to 325°F (160°C). Line two sheet pans with parchment paper.

Dust another sheet of parchment paper with flour. Working with one piece of dough at a time, place it on the floured parchment, cover with its plastic wrap, and roll until it's about ⅛ inch (6 mm) thick. Use a 3-inch (7.5 cm) cookie cutter to cut out as many rounds as possible. Use a 1½- or 2-inch (4 or 5 cm) cutter to cut out small rounds from the center of half of them. Transfer to the prepared sheet pans, spacing them at least 1 inch (2.5 cm) apart. Gather the dough scraps, roll out again, and cut more rounds and doughnut-shaped cookies. (Each time you gather and reroll the scraps, the marble pattern will become darker and more homogeneous—use good spatial awareness skills to cut as many cookies as possible the first time.)

Bake until lightly golden, 16 to 18 minutes, switching racks and rotating the sheets front to back about halfway through.

Just before serving, spread a small spoonful of jam onto the flat sides of the rounds. Top with the doughnut-shaped cookies and dust with powdered sugar.

Do Ahead The cookie dough can be made up to 3 days in advance of serving, wrapped tightly in plastic, and stored in the refrigerator. The jam filling does start to soften the baked cookie beneath it after a few hours, and the cookies taste best and crispest the day you've spread them with jam. To avoid mushy cookies, you can bake them up to 2 days in advance and, once they are completely cool, store them in an airtight container at room temperature. Then just spread with jam and dust with sugar the day you plan to serve them.

Churro Doughnuts with Chocolate Glaze

Makes 12 doughnuts

You'll need a specialty doughnut pan for this recipe to get that proper hole-in-the-middle shape, but not to worry if you don't happen to have one. The batter can also be baked in a regular muffin tin—just keep a closer eye on the muffins (which look kind of like giant doughnut holes!) as they cook, adjusting the baking time as necessary.

DOUGHNUTS

Softened butter, for the pans

1¾ cups (220 g) all-purpose flour

1½ teaspoons baking powder

2 teaspoons ground cinnamon

½ teaspoon fine sea salt

1 stick (4 ounces/115 g) unsalted butter, at room temperature

½ cup packed (105 g) brown sugar

½ cup (100 g) granulated sugar

2 large eggs

½ cup (120 ml) whole milk

2 teaspoons pure vanilla extract

GLAZE

1 cup (125 g) powdered sugar

⅓ cup (25 g) unsweetened cocoa powder

3 tablespoons whole milk or water, plus more as needed

½ teaspoon pure vanilla extract

Pinch of ground cinnamon

Pinch of fine sea salt

Make the doughnuts: Preheat the oven to 350°F (180°C). Butter two 6-hole doughnut pans.

In a medium bowl, whisk together the flour, baking powder, cinnamon, and salt.

In a stand mixer fitted with the paddle, beat the butter, brown sugar, and granulated sugar until fluffy and lightened in color, 3 to 5 minutes. Use a rubber spatula to scrape the sides and bottom of the bowl. Add the eggs one at a time, beating well after each addition. Gently mix in the flour mixture, milk, and vanilla on low speed.

Transfer the batter to a piping bag or plastic bag with one corner snipped and pipe into the prepared pans, dividing it evenly among the holes.

Bake until golden brown and a toothpick inserted into the thick part of a doughnut comes out clean, 12 to 15 minutes, rotating the pans front to back about halfway through. ⟶

Meanwhile, make the glaze: In a medium bowl, whisk together the powdered sugar, cocoa powder, milk, vanilla, cinnamon, and salt. The glaze should be thick but pourable. If it's too thick, stir in more milk, 1 tablespoon at a time, until the consistency is correct. Set aside.

Allow the doughnuts to cool in their pans for about 5 minutes, then transfer them to a wire rack. Dip the tops of the doughnuts in the chocolate glaze, return them to the rack, and let the glaze set before serving.

Do Ahead These taste best the day they are baked. You can get ahead by making them in the morning and keeping them at room temperature, uncovered so the glaze doesn't get messed up, until you're ready to serve them later that evening.

A CASE FOR OUTSOURCING DESSERT

When you host a party, guests will want to know if they can bring anything. It is 100 percent your call—you get to decide! If the offer sounds helpful, say yes. If you'd rather plan and make everything yourself, power to you. People really do want to lend a hand when they can, so don't be afraid to request something ultraspecific like for someone to bring a bouquet of flowers, a bag of crushed ice for cocktails, or a certain type of wine. Of all the courses in a menu, dessert is arguably the best to outsource. Lots of people love baking and would be thrilled to contribute by bringing a homemade sweet. As the host, it's also important to know yourself—we can't all be the best at every aspect of entertaining. So for all the nonbakers out there, consider picking up a special treat from a local bakery or ice cream parlor. Maybe your city has a beloved treat like chocolate-tahini cookies from that one lunch take-out spot or tiny buckwheat sandies from the cheese shop. A party is a chance to share your favorite over-the-top desserts with your friends.

Petits Pots de Crème au Café

Serves 6 to 8

A dessert that can be made and served in individual vessels is perfect for hosting. Pots de crème are little French custard cups that are often flavored with chocolate. And café crème is the name given to strong coffee with a splash of warm, foamy milk mixed in. This dessert combines the best of both those worlds by adding a touch of espresso powder to the chocolate pudding, and it ends up tasting like mocha. The goal texture here is super-creamy, jiggly pudding that isn't anywhere near as set as Jell-O but has a little more heft than whipped cream. Espresso cups are the ideal vessels to hold these small but potent puddings.

½ cup (120 ml) whole milk

2½ cups (600 ml) heavy cream

5 ounces (140 g) bittersweet chocolate, chopped, plus more, very finely chopped, for serving

6 large egg yolks

¼ cup (50 g) sugar

1 tablespoon instant espresso powder

2 teaspoons pure vanilla extract

¼ teaspoon fine sea salt

Preheat the oven to 325°F (160°C).

In a medium saucepan, bring the milk and 2 cups (480 ml) of the cream to a simmer over medium heat. Remove from the heat, add the chopped chocolate, and whisk until the chocolate melts.

In a medium bowl, stir together the egg yolks and sugar. Whisk continuously while slowly pouring in the hot chocolate mixture. Add the espresso powder, vanilla, and salt. Strain through a fine-mesh sieve into a liquid measuring cup.

Pour the strained mixture into any kind of tiny cups you have, such as espresso cups or little ramekins. Set the cups in a roasting pan and carefully add enough hot tap water to the roasting pan so that the water comes about halfway up the sides of the cups. Loosely cover the pan with foil.

Bake the puddings until their edges are set but their centers are still a little bit jiggly when nudged, 35 to 40 minutes if using espresso cups and 45 to 55 minutes if using 6-ounce ramekins.

Remove the cups from the water bath, let cool to room temperature, and then chill in the refrigerator for at least 3 hours and up to 3 days. ⟶

Just before serving, whip the remaining ½ cup (120 ml) cream. Spoon a little whipped cream on top of each pudding, garnish with finely chopped chocolate, and serve chilled.

Do Ahead You can make the espresso cups up to 3 days ahead of your party and then top with a dollop of whipped cream and a sprinkle of finely chopped chocolate just before serving. If the party is an intimate gathering, you can engage your guests in making the whipped cream (a hosting tip I learned from food writer Bee Wilson!). At the table before dessert, pass around a whisk and a big bowl filled with the cream and give everyone a turn to help whip the cream.

Dulce de Leche Gelato Affogato

Makes about 1 quart (1 L) gelato / enough to serve 8

Serving affogato is a genius party trick to keep up your sleeve. Everyone will love the pageantry of pouring hot coffee over cold ice cream at the table, and you can even let guests pour their own. (Go for a decaf coffee to ensure everyone can sleep that night!) You as the host don't really need to do much other than pull some ice cream out of the freezer and brew coffee. But if you want to go the extra mile, try making this dulce de leche gelato, which is wonderfully unexpected and delightful in an affogato.

2 cups (480 ml) whole milk

1 cup (240 ml) heavy cream

1 tablespoon ground cinnamon

¼ teaspoon fine sea salt

1½ cups (455 g) dulce de leche

1 teaspoon pure vanilla extract

2 cups (480 ml) hot decaf espresso or very strong decaf coffee

In a medium saucepan, combine the milk, cream, cinnamon, and salt. Bring to a simmer over medium heat. Add the dulce de leche and vanilla and whisk until completely incorporated.

Transfer the mixture to an airtight container and refrigerate until thoroughly chilled, at least 4 hours or up to 2 days.

Pour the chilled mixture into an ice cream maker and churn according to the manufacturer's instructions. Pack the gelato into a container, cover, and freeze until firm.

Place serving bowls (this is enough for 8 small servings) in the freezer to get very cold and frosty.

Just before serving, brew the espresso or strong coffee. Scoop about ½ cup (75 g) dulce de leche gelato into each chilled bowl. Drizzle about ¼ cup (60 ml) hot espresso into each bowl and serve immediately. (Better yet, pour the espresso over the gelato at the table!)

Do Ahead You can churn the gelato up to 1 week ahead. Make sure you pack it into an airtight container, with very little empty space in the container. You can even place a piece of parchment paper directly on the gelato before closing the container, which will help prevent ice crystals from forming.

Tiny Ice Cream Waffle Cones

Makes about 20 tiny waffle cones

When you're at an ice cream shop, there's only one correct answer to the question "Cup or cone?" Cone all the way! When having ice cream at home, a cone feels just a little more special and fun than a plain bowl—especially if your ice cream cones are adorably miniature, like these. Making waffle cones at home is actually pretty simple (although you do need a waffle cone iron), and once you've tasted a homemade waffle cone, fresh and still warm from the iron, you'll be spoiled forever.

⅔ cup (83 g) all-purpose flour, sifted

¼ teaspoon fine sea salt

3 large egg whites

¼ cup (50 g) granulated sugar, plus more for holding the cones

¼ cup packed (55 g) brown sugar

3 tablespoons whole milk

2 tablespoons hazelnut oil or vegetable oil

1 teaspoon pure vanilla extract

¼ teaspoon baking soda

Neutral oil spray

3½ ounces (100 g) bittersweet chocolate, chopped

Store-bought ice cream of your choice (try nocciola gelato!), for serving

Turn on a waffle cone maker to preheat at medium for about 15 minutes.

Meanwhile, in a small bowl, combine the flour and salt. Set aside.

In a medium bowl, combine the egg whites, granulated sugar, brown sugar, milk, hazelnut oil, vanilla, and baking soda. Whisk vigorously until thoroughly blended, about 1 minute. Add the flour mixture and whisk to incorporate.

Let the batter rest at room temperature for about 10 minutes. Fill a shallow container with about 1 inch (2.5 cm) of granulated sugar.

Spray the plates of the waffle cone maker with neutral oil, then spoon a little less than 1 tablespoon of batter into the center and use a small offset spatula to spread it evenly. Close the lid and cook for 1 minute before lifting the lid to check for doneness. You may need to cook the waffle cone for another minute or so, depending on your machine and the heat setting. When it's golden brown all over, quickly remove the waffle from the hot plate and wrap it around the cone shaper that comes with the machine. Hold it in place until set, then stick the cone in the sugar as if it were an umbrella on the beach. Repeat to cook and shape the remaining waffle cones.

Melt the chocolate either in a double boiler or in a microwave-safe bowl in the microwave in consecutive 10-second bursts. Dribble a little melted chocolate into each waffle cone and tilt the cone so that the chocolate covers the bottom inch or so. Replace it in the sugar sand, upright again.

When the waffle cones are completely cool and the chocolate has hardened, place the cones in an airtight container and store at room temperature until ready to serve.

To serve, scoop some ice cream into each cone and eat right away.

Gingersnap and Lemon Ice Cream Sandwiches

Makes 10 ice cream sandwiches

Kids and adults alike will go wild for these ice cream sandwiches. The combo of lemon and ginger tastes perfectly refreshing on a hot summer day but is truly delightful year-round. Store-bought lemon ice cream makes these doable for even large parties.

2 cups (250 g) all-purpose flour

1½ teaspoons baking soda

1 teaspoon cream of tartar

¾ cup (150 g) granulated sugar

1 stick (4 ounces/113 g) unsalted butter, melted

6 tablespoons (90 ml) molasses

2 tablespoons vegetable oil

1 large egg

2 teaspoons ground ginger

2 teaspoons ground cinnamon

¾ teaspoon fine sea salt

Demerara sugar, for sprinkling

2½ cups (375 g) store-bought lemon ice cream, softened slightly at room temperature

Position racks in the top and center of the oven and preheat the oven to 325°F (160°C). Line three sheet pans with parchment paper.

In a medium bowl, whisk together the flour, baking soda, and cream of tartar.

In a large bowl, combine the granulated sugar, melted butter, molasses, vegetable oil, egg, ginger, cinnamon, and salt. Whisk until thoroughly blended. Add the flour mixture and use a rubber spatula to fold it in until no flour streaks remain.

Scoop out 20 balls of cookie dough, each about 2 tablespoons, and place them on the prepared sheet pans, evenly spaced. Sprinkle generously with demerara sugar.

Bake two sheets at a time until the cookie tops are crackled and the edges are slightly darker brown, 10 to 15 minutes, switching racks and rotating the sheets front to back about halfway through.

Let cool on the pans for 5 minutes, then transfer to a wire rack to cool completely. Bake the third sheet of cookies the same way.

Scoop about ¼ cup (40 g) of lemon ice cream on the flat side of one cookie and use a table knife or offset spatula to spread it out to cover the entire cookie. Sandwich another ginger cookie on top, with the flat side touching the ice cream. Wrap tightly with parchment paper, place in an airtight container, and freeze until firm, at least 1 hour, before serving.

Do Ahead The gingersnap cookies can be baked up to 2 days ahead and stored, once they are completely cool, in an airtight container at room temperature. The finished ice cream sandwiches will keep in the freezer for up to 1 week. If you plan to freeze them for longer than a few hours before serving, make sure they are tightly wrapped. You might want to double-wrap them in two sheets of parchment and then, just before serving, remove the wrapping to make them look cute.

SPAGHETTATA

There's one notable exception to the usual practice of offering sweet nibbleable bites at the end of a meal: spaghettata—a boisterous Italian ritual of serving generous plates of steaming hot pasta to friends late in the night (or early hours of the morning) after you've all partied to your heart's content, are maybe a little tipsy, and don't want the fun to end.

Spaghettata works especially well as an after-party. If you're all out at a bar, invite friends to come back to your place and put a pot of salted water on to boil. For every four people, cook a 1-pound (500 g) box of spaghetti (or whichever shape of dried pasta you happen to have) until it's al dente. In a large skillet, warm a few tablespoons each of butter and extra-virgin olive oil over medium heat until the butter melts, then add several cloves of thinly sliced garlic, a few anchovies if you like them, a pinch of red pepper flakes, and 2 pinches of fennel seeds. Cook, stirring, until the garlic softens and turns golden. Drain the noodles, stir them directly into the garlic mixture, and serve hot, topped with lots of grated Parmigiano-Reggiano cheese.

Buon appetito! Your friends will love you forever.

All About Flowers

Fresh flowers always mean celebration, whether for a birthday, anniversary, new babe on the way, or any other special event. You can create an artful, gorgeous arrangement at home. Here are a few simple tips to keep in mind when arranging flowers:

1 **Tall blooms for standing spaces and short (or trimmed) blooms for seated spaces:** If you have an entryway table, bar cart, or somewhere people will likely be standing, choose a tall vase and long-stemmed flowers like sunflowers or gladioli. These blooms will be most striking in a space where they can stretch out. On the other hand, when you're creating an arrangement that will be placed on a dining table or low coffee table, trim the stems so that the flowers aren't too tall in their vase. You don't want to obstruct anyone's view across the table when they're seated. Test it out by sitting down in one of the chairs and making sure the flowers are no higher than your chin.

2 **Choose your vessel carefully:** Some flowers like tulips need the support of tall, straight sides. Others might require a vase with some bottom-weighted heft. And don't be afraid to think outside the box. Flowers can be arranged in all kinds of containers: ceramic vases, glass jars, water pitchers, cleaned tomato cans, empty sauerkraut jugs, and so on.

3 **Don't forget the greens:** Even the most beautiful flowers will benefit from being paired with fresh greens. When you're buying flowers, make sure to think about including a good balance of leafy green stems, too, such as eucalyptus or viburnum stems. Greens are usually much more affordable than flowers, and they make homemade arrangements feel intentional and lush.

4 **Aim for an interesting shape:** You want the overall shape of the arrangement to be visually interesting and pleasing. In other words, try to create a sense of movement within the flowers. Rather than cutting all the stems to the same height, which ends up looking boring in its sameness, trim some shorter and place those around the edges of the vase. If there's a bloom that naturally curves, find a spot where it can drape and flow.

GROCERY STORE BOUQUETS: CHOOSE MONOCHROMATIC OR COMPLEMENTARY

Fresh-cut flowers can be pricey. For the right occasion, a talented florist is definitely worth their weight in gold. But when you're on a tight budget, look no further than the flower selection at your local grocery store. Trader Joe's always has an excellent affordable selection. There's usually a wide range to choose from, but a foolproof rule is to choose monochromatic or complementary-colored flowers. Start by letting your eye wander until it lands on a flower that it likes. Now, building from that base, pair your hero flower with others that are different shades of the same color. Or go for complementary colors (i.e., two colors that oppose each other on the color wheel, like yellow and purple or red and green, for example).

NONTRADITIONAL ARRANGEMENTS

If you live somewhere with a garden or wilderness nearby, you can forage for things like blossoming branches, sprigs of bushy rosemary, and spindly twigs that make for striking and unique arrangements. Get creative with what you can find. Sturdy plants and branches often last much longer than delicate blooms. You can also consider placing groupings of beautiful found objects, like moss-covered pinecones, directly on the dining table as festive decoration.

FLOWERS AS HOST GIFTS

Flowers make a lovely host gift. If one of your guests brings you a bouquet wrapped in paper, try to get the flowers into water as soon as you can. You likely won't have the time to unwrap and arrange gifted flowers in a vase while your guests arrive, but make sure to get those stems submerged! A truly pro move is to bring flowers already arranged in a vase as a host gift.

HOW TO MAKE FLOWERS LAST

There are a few easy steps you can take to keep flowers looking their best for as long as possible.

- As soon as you get home with the flowers, untie the bouquet, letting the stems separate gently near the kitchen sink.

- Working with one stem at a time, remove any damaged petals and leaves. Decide on an approximate height for your arrangement and use floral shears or sharp scissors to trim at least ½ inch (1.3 cm) from the bottoms of the stems, making the cut on a diagonal instead of straight across. The increased surface area of a diagonal cut will allow the stem to drink up more water.

- Immediately after trimming, place the stem in a bucket of clean, cool water. (This doesn't have to be the vase you're going to use for your arrangement; the idea is just to get the freshly cut stem into water right away.)

- When you do start to put the flowers in their vase, trim any leaves that are low enough on the stems that they'll be submerged.

- To make flowers last, you should ideally change the water and trim ½ inch (1.3 cm) from the bottoms of the stems daily (or every few days if you aren't such an ambitious flower preservationist).

FLOWER FOOD

Does that little packet of flower food that comes with bouquets actually work? It does! It feeds the flowers with sugar and it prevents bacterial growth by adding a tiny bit of disinfectant to the water. If the bouquet you bought didn't come with a packet of flower food, you can make your own using ingredients that you probably already have in your home. Check out the recipe below.

DIY FLOWER FOOD

1 quart (1 L) cool water

1 tablespoon sugar

2 teaspoons lemon juice or 1 teaspoon distilled white vinegar

1 teaspoon bleach

In a vase, combine all the ingredients and stir briefly, just to dissolve the sugar.

Drinks

Gone are the days when party drinks were overly boozy, uniform, and not very delicious. The option of either red or white wine has been replaced with everything from funky, naturally fermented pét-nats to unexpectedly dark ruby-hued rosés. A good rule of thumb is to have two drink options for your guests. For example: beer and wine. Or, if you are serving a cocktail, try to have wine as well. You can suggest to your guests that they bring wines they might like. That makes less work for you, and you also might be introduced to some new favorite bottles! As the thoughtful host that you are, you'll want to offer a nonalcoholic option for guests who aren't drinking, and this chapter has plenty of recipes to choose from: Nonalcoholic Sparkling Strawberry-Rhubarb Elixir (page 250), Faux-jito (page 258), Mock Tiki Punch (page 263), and more. Fear not, if you're already making an alcoholic cocktail, you've already done half if not more of the work to create the nonalcoholic version.

Spritz

Makes 1 cocktail

A dreamy low-alcohol sparkling cocktail for summertime. The classic spritz (sometimes called the Venetian spritz) is traditionally made with Aperol and prosecco. However, there are endless variations on the theme, and it's fun to come up with your own house version. (See the variations that follow for a few ideas to get you started.)

Ice cubes

2 ounces (60 ml) orange or red bitter liqueur

3 ounces (90 ml) sparkling white wine

2 ounces (60 ml) sparkling water

1 orange half-moon

1 green olive

Fill a rocks or wine glass about three-quarters full of ice. Pour the bitter liqueur over the ice. Add the sparkling wine and water and use a long-handled spoon or straw to stir. Garnish with the orange half-moon. Skewer the olive with a cocktail pick and drop it into the drink. Serve.

Variations

BICICLETTA

For the bitter liqueur, use Campari, which has a famously strong bitterness. This drink typically uses prosecco, but any sparkling dry Italian white wine will do. Garnish with a lemon half-moon.

AMERICANO

Instead of sparkling wine, swap in sweet vermouth. Use equal parts bitter liqueur and sweet vermouth (1½ ounces/45 ml of each) and two parts (3 ounces/90 ml) sparkling water. The olive garnish is optional.

NEGRONI SBAGLIATO

This drink is *sbagliato*, which means "incorrect," because prosecco is subbed for the usual gin of a Negroni. The bubbles make it lighter—and spritzier! Use 1 ounce (30 ml) bitter liqueur, 1 ounce (30 ml) sweet vermouth, and 3 ounces (90 ml) prosecco. Garnish with only the orange, no olive.

Nonalcoholic Chinotto Spritz

Makes 4 drinks

Spritzes get their characteristic bitterness from red liqueur, so how do you go about making a nonalcoholic version of the drink? Try this recipe, which utilizes the tongue-prickling bitterness of strong, black Earl Grey tea. Chinotto, an Italian soda, plays up the citrusy notes of the tea.

2 Earl Grey tea bags

1 cup (240 ml) boiling water

Ice cubes

1 cup (240 ml) chinotto

1 cup (240 ml) sparkling water

4 orange half-moons

Place the tea bags in a mug and pour in the boiling water. Let steep for 5 minutes. Remove and discard the tea bags, using the back of a spoon to squeeze any liquid back into the mug, and chill the tea in the refrigerator until cold.

Fill four rocks or wine glasses about three-quarters full of ice. Pour 2 ounces (60 ml) of the chilled tea over the ice in each glass. Divide the chinotto and sparkling water among the glasses and use a long-handled spoon or straw to stir. Garnish with an orange half-moon. Serve.

EDIBLE FLOWER ICE CUBES

To add a beautiful touch to ice cubes for party drinks, freeze edible flowers inside the cubes. Here's how to do it: Rinse a clean, empty ice cube tray and let it drip-dry for just a moment, so it's still a little wet. Place an edible flower (such as a viola, marigold, nasturtium, bachelor's button, citrus blossom, rose, lavender, anise hyssop, etc.) in the bottom of each cube, pressing gently to adhere the petals to the tray. Gently dribble enough cool water in each cube to just cover the flower. Freeze until solid. The flower should be frozen in place at the bottom of the cube. If it floated up to the surface, simply flip it over. Pour in more water to top up each cube and freeze again until solid. Remember, as always when cooking with edible flowers, choose blooms that haven't been sprayed with pesticides or harmful chemicals.

Nonalcoholic Raspberry-Lime Spritz

Makes 4 drinks

The wonderful thing about homemade soda is you can customize its sweetness level to your liking. For sweeter drinks, simply add a little more syrup to each glass. If you'd like the drink to be more tart, mix in an extra splash of lime juice.

2 cups (240 g) fresh or
    (500 g) frozen raspberries

¾ cup (150 g) sugar

¾ cup (180 ml) water

2 limes

Ice cubes

Sparkling water

In a medium saucepan, combine the raspberries, sugar, water, and finely grated zest of the limes. (Set aside the zested limes.) Bring to a simmer over medium-low heat and cook, stirring occasionally, until the raspberries soften and collapse on themselves, 5 to 8 minutes. Strain the mixture through a fine-mesh sieve into a jar and let cool to room temperature.

Fill four tall straight-sided glasses with ice cubes. Divide the cooled syrup among the glasses. Add 1 teaspoon of lime juice to each glass and top up with sparkling water. Use a long-handled spoon to stir before serving.

Nonalcoholic Sparkling Strawberry-Rhubarb Elixir

Makes about 2 cups elixir / enough for 16 drinks

What makes this drink an elixir? It has tonifying rhubarb (to restore and increase your energy), probiotic-rich kombucha (for your digestion), and, as an optional addition, a magnesium supplement, which can be especially helpful in supporting women's health. On top of all that, it just tastes great, too.

1 pound (450 g) strawberries, hulled, plus strawberry slices for garnish

12 ounces (340 g) rhubarb, chopped

1 cup (240 ml) water

½ cup (100 g) sugar

Ice cubes

6 cups (1.4 L) pomegranate kombucha

Powdered magnesium supplement (optional)

Sparkling water

In a medium stainless-steel saucepan, combine the strawberries, rhubarb, water, and sugar. Bring to a simmer over medium-high heat and cook, stirring occasionally, until the fruit collapses in complete tenderness, about 10 minutes. Strain the syrup through a fine-mesh sieve and store in a jar in the fridge for up to 1 week.

For one drink, half fill a rocks glass with ice. Pour 1 ounce (30 ml) of strawberry-rhubarb syrup over the ice. Add 3 ounces (90 ml) of kombucha, 1 teaspoon magnesium (if using), and enough sparkling water to top up the glass. Garnish with a strawberry slice before serving.

Shandy

Makes 1 drink

Beer is already refreshing on its own, but if you'd like to try something new, how about mixing equal parts beer and sparkling lemonade for a drink called a shandy? Actually, shandies aren't new at all; they've been around since at least the late nineteenth century, when legend has it an innkeeper invented the drink because he needed to stretch his beer stash to accommodate his thirsty customers, many of whom were cyclists riding along the country roads. Shandies are ideal drinks to serve at daytime parties because they're low-ABV and customizable. And if you don't think you like beer, give a shandy a shot and it might change your mind. Guests can add the beer and lemonade in whatever proportion they'd like.

¾ cup (180 ml) sparkling lemonade, chilled

¾ cup (180 ml) light lager or pilsner beer, chilled

Lemon twist or wheel (see Twists and Twirls, page 253)

In a chilled tall glass, combine the sparkling lemonade and beer. Garnish with the lemon twist and serve.

Variations

ROCK SHANDY

Use a nonalcoholic beer for an entirely booze-free drink.

RADLER*

Use sparkling grapefruit soda instead of sparkling lemonade and choose a German-style beer like hefeweizen. Garnish with a grapefruit twist or half-moon.

MONACO

Opt for lager and add a colorful dash of grenadine.

Radler is German for "cyclist."

TWISTS AND TWIRLS

A lemon twist is an iconic cocktail garnish. To impress your friends, you'll want to know how to properly make one. Try using other citrus fruits like blood orange, grapefruit, or lime, too.

SPIRAL

There is a specific tool (called a channel knife) for this job that you might have seen in a bar. It looks like a tiny V-shaped blade on a handle, and when you drag it around a lemon, it'll cut a thin strip of zest, which can be curled around a chopstick into a tight spiral.

THIN TWIRL

Use a paring knife to cut a lemon in half and then cut a thin round slice from the middle. Next, use the tip of the knife to cut right where the yellow peel meets the white pith, working your way all the way around the perimeter of the round. You should now have a thin O-shaped peel and a round of rind-less fruit. Save the rind-less fruit piece for another recipe. Cut the peel circle to create a long strip, then curl it tightly around your finger or a chopstick.

BASIC TWIST

A vegetable peeler is surprisingly perfect for cutting lemon peel twists. Hold the peeler firmly in your hand but press it gently against the fruit so that you remove a strip of fragrant yellow zest and very little of the bitter white pith. Give it a little twist and voilà!

Classic Martini

Makes 1 cocktail

A martini is arguably the cocktail-iest cocktail of them all, and often it's very personal—some people prefer gin while others absolutely insist on vodka. You can have loads of fun and live out your wildest bartender dreams at a party by mixing individual drinks for guests (and trying all the variations that follow). Traditionally, martinis are stirred, not shaken, although the vodka martini is the exception. And important to note, always use an odd number of olives in a dirty martini—an even number of garnishes on a cocktail is seen as bad luck! Whichever way you serve the martini, make sure to chill the glass in the freezer ahead of time so that it is pristinely cold.

2 ounces (60 ml) gin

1 ounce (30 ml) dry vermouth

2 dashes orange bitters

Ice cubes

1 strip of lemon peel (see Twists and Twirls, page 253)

Chill a coupe or cocktail glass in the freezer until frosty.

In a mixing glass, combine the gin, dry vermouth, and bitters. Add enough ice to halfway fill the mixing glass and stir until thoroughly chilled, about 20 seconds, so that the liquids mix and chill but the ice doesn't get the chance to dilute the drink. Strain into the chilled glass. Hold the lemon peel over the glass, yellow side facing the drink, and twist to release the fragrant oils, then drop the peel into the glass or balance it on the rim. Serve.

Variations

DIRTY MARTINI

Add a splash of olive brine when you add the bitters. For garnish, instead of the lemon peel, skewer 1 or 3 green olives on a cocktail pick and drop it into the glass just before serving. (See also Customizable Skewers, page 262.)

50/50 MARTINI

Use equal parts gin and dry vermouth (1½ ounces/45 ml of each per drink) and follow the main recipe. →

DRY MARTINI

Use a 3:1 ratio of gin to dry vermouth: 2¼ ounces gin and ¾ ounce dry vermouth (or 75 ml gin and 25 ml dry vermouth) per drink. You can garnish with your choice of either a lemon twist or a green olive on a cocktail pick.

VODKA MARTINI

In a cocktail shaker, combine 2¼ ounces vodka and ¾ ounce dry vermouth (or 75 ml vodka and 25 ml dry vermouth). Add 2 dashes of orange bitters and enough ice to fill the shaker halfway, cover, and shake vigorously for 15 seconds. Strain into a chilled coupe or cocktail glass. Garnish with 1 or 3 green olives on a cocktail pick.

FRUIT-TINI MIX-INS

The Appletini was wildly popular during the 1990s, and although it has been teased, there's nothing wrong with adding some fruit to your drink. The key is to not go overboard—a little splash is all it takes.

Pomegranatini: Add 1 teaspoon pomegranate syrup when you add the bitters to the Classic Martini (page 254) or Vodka Martini (above) and follow the recipe from there. Garnish with a lemon (or other citrus fruit) twist.

Sour Cherry-tini: Add 1 teaspoon sour cherry jam when you add the bitters to the Vodka Martini (above) and follow the recipe from there. Garnish with a lemon (or other citrus fruit) twist.

Black Currantini: Add 1 tablespoon crème de cassis when you add the bitters to the Classic Martini (page 254) or Vodka Martini (above) and follow the recipe from there. Garnish with a lemon (or other citrus fruit) twist.

Rosemary Gin and Tonic

Makes 1 cocktail

If you want to serve a cocktail at your party but aren't sure what your guests like, a G&T is a safe bet. Gin has layers upon layers of botanical aromas, so it seems only appropriate to make a rosemary-infused gin and tonic. If you don't happen to have access to fresh rosemary where you live, try a different fresh woodsy herb like thyme or bay.

Ice cubes

2 ounces (60 ml) gin

4 ounces (120 ml) tonic water

1 sprig fresh rosemary

1 lime wheel

Fill a tall straight-sided glass with ice cubes. Pour in the gin and tonic water and use a long-handled spoon or straw to stir. Thwack the rosemary sprig on the countertop, then garnish the drink with it and the lime wheel. Serve.

Faux-jito

Makes 8 drinks

This one is wonderful for warm-weather parties of all kinds. Classic mojitos combine rum, tart lime, and cooling mint for a drink that's thirst-quenching and revivifying. You can make an impressive nonalcoholic version by leaving out the rum and adjusting the amounts of the other ingredients.

½ cup (100 g) sugar

1 lime, plus 8 lime wheels for garnish

½ cup (120 ml) water

8 sprigs fresh mint, plus more
  for garnish

1 cup (240 ml) fresh lime juice

Ice cubes

Chilled sparkling water

Place the sugar in a small saucepan. Finely grate the zest of the whole lime directly over the sugar, letting the zest fall into the pan. Use your fingertips to rub the zest into the sugar until fragrant, about 1 minute. Pour in the water and bring to a boil, stirring to dissolve the sugar. As soon as all the sugar dissolves, remove the pan from the heat, strain the simple syrup into a jar, and let cool to room temperature.

For one drink, muddle a mint sprig in the bottom of a cocktail shaker using a muddler or the handle of a wooden spoon. Add 1 ounce (30 ml) of the lime juice, a handful of ice cubes, and ½ ounce (15 ml) of the simple syrup. Shake until chilled, then strain into a tall glass filled with ice. Top up the glass with a splash of sparkling water. Garnish with a lime wheel and extra mint. Serve.

Frozen Margarita

Makes 4 cocktails

It's hard to find someone who doesn't like a margarita . . . but a frozen margarita? Who wouldn't love a boozy slushie? You can make a round of frozen margaritas using nothing but a blender in less than a minute. Try the sweet strawberry variation below and have fun with the salt rim garnish. Margaritas are obviously fantastic with Mexican food, but if I'm being honest, I love a margarita any day! This one would be brilliant alongside Fish Kebabs (page 141).

Lime wedge and flaky salt, for rimming
  the glass (optional)

¾ cup (180 ml) blanco tequila

½ cup (120 ml) Cointreau

½ cup (120 ml) fresh lime juice

2 tablespoons agave syrup

Finely grated zest of 1 lime

4 cups (560 g) crushed ice

Prepare four glasses: If you'd like salt rims, moisten half the rim of each glass with a lime wedge, then dip the moistened rim in flaky salt.

In a blender, combine the tequila, Cointreau, lime juice, agave, lime zest, and crushed ice. Blend until slushy, about 30 seconds. Divide the frozen margarita among the prepared glasses.

Variation

FROZEN STRAWBERRY MARGARITA

Add 2 cups (300 g) frozen strawberries to the blender and use only 2 cups (280 g) crushed ice. Garnish with fresh strawberry slices. If you like, mix a sprinkle of Tajín into the flaky salt for the rims.

Mai Tai Punch

Serves 8

When you see a punch bowl at a party, you know it's going to be a good time. Don't skip the garnishes—a tropical drink tastes best with a cocktail umbrella affixed to it.

1 cup (240 ml) fresh lime juice

1 cup (240 ml) aged rum

¾ cup (180 ml) orgeat syrup

½ cup (120 ml) gold rum

½ cup (120 ml) rhum agricole blanc

½ cup (120 ml) orange liqueur (orange Curaçao, Grand Marnier, or Cointreau)

Ice cubes

2 limes, thinly sliced into wheels

2 oranges, thinly sliced and cut into half-wheels

1 grapefruit, thinly sliced and cut into half-wheels

Crushed ice (optional)

8 pineapple slices, for garnish

8 bushy fresh mint sprigs, for garnish

Cocktail umbrellas

Pour the lime juice, aged rum, orgeat, gold rum, rhum agricole blanc, and orange liqueur into a large glass jar or jug. Use a long-handled spoon to stir. Cover and chill in the refrigerator until you're ready to serve.

Transfer the chilled mai tai mixture to a punch bowl filled with ice cubes. Add the lime, orange, and grapefruit wheels, letting them float.

Fill each glass with ice (crushed is best here, but feel free to use cubes if that's what you have on hand) and then pour the mai tai punch over the ice. Garnish each drink with any combination of a pineapple slice, a sprig of mint, and/or a cocktail umbrella. Serve.

Variations

MANGO TAI

Add 1 cup (240 ml) mango juice (look for a store-bought bottle that's 100 percent juice with no added sugar) when you add the lime juice.

POG TAI

Add 1 cup (240 ml) POG (passion fruit–orange–guava) juice when you add the lime juice.

CUSTOMIZABLE SKEWERS

You know those little hangtags that people put around the stems of wine glasses at parties to distinguish their glass from others? Very hard not to look silly with one of those, right? What is undeniably more appealing and fun is letting your guests make their own personalized skewer for their drink. Then, if you need to identify your drink, you can say something like, "Mine is the one with the olive, pickle, and chile." And you could even make it a game to guess which friend has which drink based on their choice of garnish. Simply set out plenty of cocktail picks and a platter or small bowls of various skewerable things.

For savory cocktails (such as Rosemary Gin and Tonic, page 257, or Classic Martini, page 254), try:

- pitted green olives (try the jumbo kind stuffed with pimiento or, for people who say they're not "olive people," offer them Castelvetrano)

- pickled pearl onions

- long, thin strips of cucumber that can be threaded onto the cocktail pick

- cornichons or other small pickles

- hot Calabrian chile peppers

- cherry tomatoes

For sweet or fruity cocktails (such as Mai Tai Punch, page 260, or Frozen Margarita, page 259), try:

- frozen raspberries

- halved or quartered strawberries

- fresh pineapple pieces

- Amarena cherries

Mock Tiki Punch

Serves 8

One winning hosting strategy is to make this fruity, nonalcoholic punch and allow guests to add a splash of rum if they want by including a bottle on the side, with a shot glass or jigger for those who like to be more precise in their measuring. That way, you have both a nonalcoholic and alcoholic option and you've prepared only one thing. This mock tiki punch includes orgeat, a super-fragrant nonalcoholic cocktail syrup made from almonds and often flavored with floral essences like rose water. Grenadine, another nonalcoholic bar syrup, imparts its ruby red color to the punch. See if you can find a grenadine that doesn't have any artificial coloring or high-fructose corn syrup. These days, there are many craft producers making real grenadine from pomegranate juice.

1¼ cups (300 ml) pineapple juice (look for one that is 100% juice)

1¼ cups (300 ml) fresh orange juice

½ cup (120 ml) orgeat

1-liter bottle lemon-lime soda

2 limes, thinly sliced into wheels

2 oranges, thinly sliced and cut into half-wheels

Grenadine

Crushed ice

8 pineapple slices, for garnish

8 bushy fresh mint sprigs, for garnish

Cocktail umbrellas

Pour the pineapple juice, orange juice, and orgeat into a large glass jar or jug. Use a long-handled spoon to stir. Cover and chill in the refrigerator until you're ready to serve.

Transfer the chilled mock tiki mixture to a punch bowl and stir in the lemon-lime soda. Add the lime and orange wheels, letting them float.

Drizzle a splash of grenadine into each glass, fill with crushed ice, and gently pour in the mock tiki punch. Garnish each drink with any combination of a pineapple slice, a sprig of mint, and/or a cocktail umbrella. Serve.

Negroni Pitcher

Serves 12

The only thing better than one perfect Negroni is a pitcher full of Negronis: ideal for a big party and easy to make ahead. Chill the mixture in the fridge for as long as needed, but wait to add any ice, which will dilute the cocktail, until just before serving.

1½ cups (360 ml) gin

1½ cups (360 ml) red bitter liqueur

1½ cups (360 ml) sweet red vermouth

Ice cubes

Orange, for garnish

In a pitcher or large bottle, combine the gin, red bitter liqueur, and sweet vermouth. Cover and refrigerate until thoroughly chilled, at least 4 hours.

For each drink, fill a short glass with ice cubes. Pour the chilled Negroni mixture over the ice. Using a small knife or vegetable peeler, cut a long narrow strip of orange zest, pressing the blade lightly to avoid the bitter white pith. Twist the peel into a curlicue over the glass, then drop it into the drink. Serve.

Glühwein

Serves 6

Feel free to switch up the spices in this mulled wine to your liking. Cardamom pods would be terrific, as would a few whole cloves pressed right into the orange and lemon peels. You can also adjust the amount of sugar to suit the particular wine you use. Choose a bottle that's not too fancy or precious.

2 cinnamon sticks

1 whole star anise

8 juniper berries

⅓ cup packed (70 g) brown sugar

1 cup (240 ml) water

1 (750 ml) bottle dry red wine

1 orange, thinly sliced

½ lemon, thinly sliced

In a heavy-bottomed pot, combine the cinnamon sticks, star anise, juniper, brown sugar, and water. Cook over medium heat, stirring until the sugar dissolves. Turn the heat to very low and add the wine, orange slices, and lemon slices. Keep the heat very low—you don't want the wine to bubble at all, otherwise the alcohol will cook off—and let the wine mull for about 30 minutes.

To serve, ladle hot glühwein into glasses or mugs, leaving the whole spices behind but adding an orange slice or two to each glass.

PARTY FOUL: SPILLED RED WINE

First and most important, don't panic. Spills happen. Act as quickly as you can; the longer you wait, the tougher the stain will be to remove. Use a paper towel to gently blot the spill, soaking up wine without pressing too firmly. Do not scrub! Stop here if the material that the wine spilled on is dry-clean only. Next, wet a sponge or clean rag with cold water (some people like to use club soda) and use that to gently blot the spill. If you're not sure if the fabric is colorfast, you should test an inconspicuous area before proceeding with the next step. Last, sprinkle the stained area with enough baking soda to cover it completely, let it settle for a few minutes, and then vacuum it up. Voilà! (If there's still a stubborn stain, try applying a mixture of two parts hydrogen peroxide to one part liquid dish soap, letting it soak for at least 20 minutes, and then blotting clean with a wet sponge.)

THE WINE GUIDE

Here's the truth about wine: There are no rules! (Isn't that liberating?) You don't need to serve white wine with fish or red wine with red meat. You don't need a special glass to serve pinot noir. You don't even need to care about whether a wine has received ninety-nine points on some random scale. It's simple, really. You should drink wine you love. Full stop.

The best (and most delicious) way to figure out which wine you love is to taste lots of wine. Ask friends to bring over their current favorite bottle. Try local wines when you travel. In general, the wine produced in a certain region of the world will likely go well with that same region's food specialties. Think Provençal rosé with a traditional dish from Provence like a grand aioli. Or a glass of Barbera d'Alba from Italy's Piemonte region with a plate of white truffle pasta.

Some wonderful wine-producing areas to get to know include New York's Finger Lakes, California's Central Coast, and Hungary's Tokaj region. Another fun exercise is to pick a celebrated region and, instead of choosing the obvious type of wine that region is known for, try a wine from there that is less famous. For example, Northern Italian reds are considered among the finest in the world. But the white wines produced there (like Roero Arneis) are brilliant, too.

If you're curious about a type of wine, take a chance on it. Ever tasted orange wine? Or pét-nat? Go see what all the fuss is about. And befriend someone at a nearby wineshop. They'll be able to help point you in the right direction, and you never know what you may discover.

The Home Bar

Whether you have a proper bar cart or a tiny slice of kitchen counter space dedicated to drinks, you can create an intentional place for bottles, tools, and glassware. Setting up a home bar is one way to make your space reflect your style. Are you somebody who owns a vintage set of sleek highball glasses that look like they were lifted off the set of *Madmen*? Do you have a jar of Maraschino cherries or those real-deal Italian Amarena cherries in the blue-and-white crock? Proudly display your favorite goods alongside any personal touches (like your grandmother's crystal candy bowl) or seasonal decor. A bowl of brightly colored citrus in the winter brings cheer to a home bar—and the fruits will likely be used in cocktails, too. One of the best parts of a home bar is that it combines utility and design.

ALL THE BAR TOOLS

Bar tools are kind of like the jewelry of your home bar wardrobe. They're often pretty, shiny, and a pleasure to behold. They're also not strictly necessary, but they do add a special touch that makes mixing cocktails at home really fun and satisfying. Some drinks—like a Spritz (page 247) or Shandy (page 251)—can be made in the glass they're served in, while others require a shaker or a mixing glass.

Shakers come in two main styles: cobbler shakers and Boston shakers. (A third style, the French shaker, is hardly used these days.) Boston shakers are usually preferred by bartenders, and they look like two tins (or a tin and glass) that fit tightly together. These shakers might be what professionals use, but they necessitate an additional bar tool—a Hawthorne strainer—and can sometimes leak if not properly assembled. The cobbler shaker is much more user-friendly and perfectly appropriate for a home bar. It has a built-in strainer at the top, so when you pour your

shaken drink into a glass, the shaker strainer does all the work of holding back ice cubes, making sure that only the good stuff ends up in the glass. Occasionally, cobbler shaker top caps even do triple-duty as a handy 1-ounce (30 ml) measuring cup. If not, you'll need a jigger, which is shaped like an open hourglass used for measuring alcohol.

If you're making a cocktail in a mixing glass, you might like to use a long-handled bar spoon. The handle shaft spirals upward to an often counterweighted grip point that makes stirring with a bar spoon a delightful experience.

BOTTLES TO STOCK

The bottles you keep on hand are totally up to you. What do you like to drink and how much space do you have? If you're a Negroni household (see Negroni Pitcher, page 264), you'll want gin, red bitter liqueur, and sweet vermouth so that you can mix your favorite cocktail whenever you feel like it. Love to sip on mezcal? Keep a few different kinds in your home bar if that's your jam. Are you more of an old-fashioned fan? Then make sure you've got whiskey (rye or bourbon) and Angostura bitters. Remember that vermouth is perishable and should be stored in the refrigerator. Whether it's dry vermouth (for a Classic Martini, page 254) or sweet red vermouth, best to use it within a few months after opening. Consider buying the smaller bottles of vermouth and restocking with a fresh supply as needed. On a similar note, the mini cans of seltzer and tonic are an ideal size for those times when you're mixing only a few fizzy cocktails. No matter what liquor you're buying, seek out lesser-known producers who aren't adding any artificial flavors or other wacky ingredients to their bottles. They will taste the best. The wide world of spirits producers is ever expanding with new,

delicious options. The Sources section of this book (page 294) has a list of producers very much worth trying.

GLASSWARE

There are seemingly endless options for glassware: stemmed and stemless wine glasses, elegant coupes, exquisitely engraved crystal rocks glasses, paper-thin champagne flutes, tulip-shaped pints for beer, and so on. Having so many different choices sometimes makes it difficult to know which glasses you actually need at home. The secret that sellers of glassware probably don't want you to know is you can't really go wrong. You should drink from the glass that makes you happy. Of course, there are some super-specific types of glasses—like a champagne coupe or flute—that are intended for super-specific types of drinks. But aside from the obvious outliers, don't be afraid to serve wine in an antique French water glass or whatever beautiful glass you love. Some beer aficionados even prefer drinking beer from wine glasses, so be bold and go ahead and break some "rules." When the party is at your house, you get to decide what goes.

Menus

Get ready to party! There are all kinds of good reasons to celebrate, from holidays to first days of school and everything in between. I hope the following sample menus inspire gatherings big and small. Feel free to make adjustments to suit yourself and your guests. Try swapping in a gluten-free dessert like Dulce de Leche Gelato Affogato (page 236) or Petits Pots de Crème au Café (page 233). Or substitute or add a nonalcoholic drink that everyone will love such as Nonalcoholic Raspberry-Lime Spritz (page 249), maybe even with some edible flower ice cubes (see page 248). If you'd like a little more menu planning guidance, check out Creating Your Own Menu (page 192) for tips.

The Pre-Party

This is the menu for when you gather with friends before going to a party and you want to enjoy a drink and some small bites together before heading out. It's also great when you want to do something casual that doesn't require any real cooking The best drinks for this kind of gathering are low-ABV and bubbly—like a few bottles of pét-nat wine or a fizzy cocktail like a Spritz (page 247), and you can serve a Nonalcoholic Chinotto Spritz (page 248) to anyone who's not drinking alcohol. The food shouldn't be too laborious; ideally, you'll want little bowls of cherries or other seasonal fruit and some Choose-Your-Own-Adventure Spiced Nuts (page 26), plus maybe a Charcuterie and Pickles Platter (page 36), which is truly more assembling than cooking. It's maybe too early for a proper dessert, but dates, with their pits removed and replaced by manouri cheese, offer a natural sweet hint and a lovely balance to this menu, as does a drizzle of honey over fresh burrata.

Choose-Your-Own-Adventure Spiced Nuts (page 26)

Sardines and Buttered Saltines (page 22)

A bowl of cherries or other seasonal fruit

Burrata drizzled with honey

Charcuterie and Pickles Platter (page 36)

Dates, pitted and stuffed with manouri cheese

Spritz (page 247)

Nonalcoholic Chinotto Spritz (page 248)

A few bottles of pét-nat wine

The After-Party

For a party after the party, this menu is easy to pull together and satisfies those late-night cravings. Many of these recipes straddle the line between savory and sweet, like Cheese Dessert Tray (page 38) and Rosemary-Almond Salted Caramel Corn (page 29). For drinks, look to the soothing and sometimes bitter-edged amari, tonics, and digestifs. They are just the thing to settle you and your guests after a night of indulgences. You can stock everything you'll need for all the recipes in this menu at home, because an after-party menu should be doable at a moment's notice. And speaking of spontaneity, you cannot go wrong serving spaghettata (page 241).

Rosemary-Almond Salted Caramel Corn (page 29)

**A wedge of Parmigiano-Reggiano cheese,
with a small knife to break off hunks**

Your favorite tinned fish

Spaghettata (page 241)

**Grilled cheese sandwiches, hot from the pan, or
Gorgonzola-Prosciutto Toasties** (page 65)
if you have the ingredients for them on hand

Cheese Dessert Tray (page 38)

Chocolate-covered almonds

Dulce de Leche Gelato Affogato (page 236)

Peppermint tea

Amaro or another digestif

Galentine's Day

Romance is in the air and it's time to show your friends how much you adore them. This menu is the lovely mix of elegance and coziness, perfect for a night in with your best pals. Crunchy-Topped Mac 'n' Squash (page 186) is comfort food at its finest but also a little lighter than usual because squash stands in for extra cheese. For your table, pick up some assorted roses to complement the colors of the oranges and radicchio salad. And why not write a valentine for each friend? Tell them why you love them so much.

French breakfast radishes

A trio of cheeses: one soft, one firm, and one in between

Cara Cara, Hazelnut, and Ruby Chicories Salad (page 125)

Crunchy-Topped Mac 'n' Squash (page 186)

Herby Turkey Meatballs (page 164)

DMW (Dark-Milk-White) Chocolate Layer Cake (page 199)

Mixed fresh berries of your choice

Nonalcoholic Raspberry-Lime Spritz (page 249)

Provençal rosé

Springtime Luncheon

This spring or summer menu is fit for a lovely Mother's Day lunch or a bridal or baby shower. You can play up the pretty pastel colors of the food by having lots of floral arrangements on the table. Remember to save any super-fragrant blooms for an outdoor party or a tiny bathroom bouquet— only unscented flowers should be on a table with food. For any vegetarian guests, one easy trick to adapt a recipe is to make half the dish with meat and half without. Try it with Jamón and Fig Toasts (page 59). You don't need to replace the jamón with anything, but you could always add some fresh arugula if you like. All the dishes in this menu can be made ahead and would transport easily to an outdoor setting if the weather cooperates. If you're hosting a baby shower, the mama-to-be will be delighted if you serve a special nonalcoholic drink. Nonalcoholic Sparkling Strawberry-Rhubarb Elixir (page 250) looks gorgeous and festive.

Turmeric- and Beet-Pickled Deviled Eggs (page 49)

Minty Pea Soup with Crème Fraîche Swirl (page 89)

Jamón and Fig Toasts (page 59)

Slow-Roasted Steelhead Trout with Shiso Salad (page 147)

Green Bean, Watermelon Radish, and Crunchy Quinoa Salad (page 119)

Pistachio Butter Cake with Apricot and Candied Rose Petals (page 197)

Store-bought ice cream

Coastal California white wine

Nonalcoholic Sparkling Strawberry-Rhubarb Elixir (page 250)

Friends and Family Sunday Supper

Gather your family and chosen family for an Italian-inspired dinner. They'll be thrilled because who doesn't love Pasta Carbonara (page 191)? You can easily substitute gluten-free noodles if any of your guests have a sensitivity. You can also skip the meat in that dish, and it'll still taste fantastic. A cake feels right for a cozy menu like this one, but don't worry, Upside-Down Blood Orange Semolina Cake (page 202) isn't fussy at all. Try mixing the drinks ahead of time and let your family serve themselves while you put the finishing touches on the rest of the meal.

**Castelvetrano olives, warmed gently in a pan
with a drizzle of olive oil**

Extraordinary Green Leafy Salad (page 117)

Rose-Chile King Trumpet Mushrooms and Sautéed Greens (page 127)

Pasta Carbonara (page 191)

Potato Chip–Crust Chicken with Green Olive Relish (page 162)

Upside-Down Blood Orange Semolina Cake (page 202)

Store-bought chocolate truffles

Negroni Pitcher (page 264)

Nonalcoholic Chinotto Spritz (page 248)

Pack-and-Go Picnic!

A menu designed to be toted, whether to the park or even just the roof of your apartment building. Lay down a picnic blanket and remember to bring along all the party supplies you might need. Think: a bottle opener, a knife for cutting portions of Bánh Bagnat Mì with Lemongrass Tofu (page 175), disposable or reusable cups and plates, et cetera. And extra napkins are never a bad idea. Pack everything that needs to stay chilled into a cooler (or two) half-filled with ice. Warm foods like the Tiny Samosas with Minty Yogurt Dip (page 75) should be double-wrapped in foil and packed in an insulated bag. Maybe this'll be the party where you finally figure out why food eaten outdoors just tastes better.

Watermelon and lemon wedges for squeezing

Edamame on Ice with Black Vinegar Mignonette (page 44)

Vegetarian Summer Rolls with Peanut Sauce (page 93)

Bánh Bagnat Mì with Lemongrass Tofu (page 175)

Tiny Samosas with Minty Yogurt Dip (page 75)

Candied Ginger Cupcakes (page 205)

Bakery-bought cookies

Your favorite IPA in cans

Nonalcoholic Raspberry-Lime Spritz (page 249)

Game Day

Go, team! Watching the big game is always more fun when there are delicious food and drinks. I heard a rumor that this menu is lucky, too. All the winning favorites are here: chicken wings, guac, nachos, ballpark-style pretzels, bite-size sausages, and more. You can create subtle nods to the party theme without going overboard into kitschy territory—for example, try serving beers with labels that are the same color as the team you're rooting for. And for a nonalcoholic option, look for old-fashioned soda in glass bottles with colorful labels, too.

Bavarian-Style Soft Pretzels (page 69)

Broiled Bratwurst Bites (page 71)

Spicy Chicken Wings with Apricot-Honey-Chile Sauce (page 73)

Chips and guacamole

**Vegetarian Nachos with Sweet Potato,
Pintos en Adobo, and Cotija** (page 178)

Winning Chili con Carne (page 150)

Halva Choc-Chip Shortbread (page 220)

Marbled Matcha Snickerdoodles (page 221)

Old-fashioned soda in glass bottles

Beers with labels that are the team's colors

Vegetarian Feast

No meat, no problem for this menu. If you'd prefer to serve an entirely vegan feast, make a few simple swaps: Instead of Ejjeh-Inspired Frittata and Labne Sauce (page 109), try Tiny Samosas with Minty Yogurt Dip (page 75) and use a vegan yogurt (maybe a coconut-based one) for the dip recipe. The Cherry Tomato and Arugula Pesto Galette (page 103) crust relies on butter, but you can make it with a vegan butter or just use a store-bought vegan puff pastry (such as Pepperidge Farm) for the crust. Make two galettes and skip the Squash Blossom and Sweet Pepper Tart (page 181). For dessert, opt for a trio of store-bought sorbets to go with the fruit.

A crudités platter: Try a mix of small carrots in a variety of colors, radishes, and Persian (mini) cucumbers

Panelle (page 105)

Ejjeh-Inspired Frittata and Labne Sauce (page 109)

Cherry Tomato and Arugula Pesto Galette (page 103)

Squash Blossom and Sweet Pepper Tart (page 181)

Extraordinary Green Leafy Salad (page 117)

Green Bean, Watermelon Radish, and Crunchy Quinoa Salad (page 119)

Apricots, peaches, and plums, cut into two-bite wedges

Tiny Ice Cream Waffle Cones (page 238)

Orange wine

Lemon verbena iced tea

Hawaiian Hangout

Capture the island spirit on a plate of Slow-Cooked Pork in Cabbage Leaf Cups (page 169) or in a glass of Mai Tai Punch (page 260). The nonalcoholic option of Mock Tiki Punch (page 263) looks like a tropical sunset with its drizzle of red grenadine. And what says "It's time to party!" better than a giant punch bowl?

Edamame on Ice with Black Vinegar Mignonette (page 44)

Spicy Chicken Wings with Apricot-Honey-Chile Sauce (page 73)

Store-bought macaroni salad

Hawaiian bread rolls

Slow-Cooked Pork in Cabbage Leaf Cups (page 169)

Steamed white rice

Furikake Kabocha Moons (page 185)

Chilled mango and pineapple slices

Ube Amaretti Cookies (page 227)

Mai Tai Punch (page 260)

Mock Tiki Punch (page 263)

A selection of low-ABV, island-style beers

Taco Night

Not limited to only Tuesdays, a taco menu makes for a fun, interactive party, with guests assembling their own tacos and jostling to reach across the table for lime wedges to squeeze. The side dishes in this menu also work exceptionally well as taco fillings or toppings. Blistered Padrón Peppers on Avocado Crema (page 133) in a taco, anyone? Those peppers and the avocado crema that goes with them are a nice vegan taco filling option. The crema tastes as creamy as yogurt, but it's made without any dairy. For serving size, you can count on at least 3 tortillas per person (or 6 per person, if you're stacking 2 tortillas for each taco). And pick up one more bag of tortilla chips than you think you'll need. You don't want to run out of tortilla chips when there's pico de gallo and mango salsa on the table.

Tortilla chips and pico de gallo

Avocado slices sprinkled with flaky salt

Blistered Padrón Peppers on Avocado Crema (page 133)

**Vegetarian Nachos with Sweet Potato,
Pintos en Adobo, and Cotija** (page 178)

Tacos al Pastor (page 173)

Homemade Tortillas and Mango Salsa (page 47)

Churro Doughnuts with Chocolate Glaze (page 231)

Lime-flavored sparkling water

Frozen Margarita (page 259)

The Promotion Party

Just received a big work bonus or feeling ready to spoil your friend after their latest career achievement? This is the menu for just that occasion, with all the ritzy foods and drinks! Break out your finest glassware and tableware—champagne and oysters on the half shell practically demand it and won't settle for anything less. Vegetarian guests will love Saffron Arancini (page 79), although you should consider swapping the grated Parmigiano-Reggiano for another similar firm cheese because some vegetarians do not eat cheeses made with rennet. And for anyone who doesn't eat gluten, make sure to roll the arancini in gluten-free panko bread crumbs. Celebrating your own successes with others by your side makes the joy so much sweeter.

Champagne

Rosemary Gin and Tonic (page 257)

Oysters on the half shell

Charcuterie and Pickles Platter (page 36)

Extra-Sharp White Cheddar Seeded Crackers (page 31)

Saffron Arancini (page 79)

Watercress drizzled with fresh lemon juice and extra-virgin olive oil

Kumquat-Crab Cakes with Dill Rémoulade (page 145)

Bavette with Chimichurri (page 153)

Barley and Salted Caramel Pine Nut Tart (page 211)

Holiday Dinner Party

Here's an extravagant feast that will easily serve twelve people or more. Feel free to shorten this menu by crossing off as many dishes or drinks as you see fit. But try to preserve a nice balance to the meal by keeping the proportion of starters to mains to sides to desserts about the same. Also, keep in mind any needs of your guests. Will a vegetarian be joining your party? A hearty dish like Green Bean, Watermelon Radish, and Crunchy Quinoa Salad (page 119) or Saffron Couscous with Cauliflower, Chickpeas, and Pomegranate (page 114) would be much appreciated. Sometimes the very best desserts are the simplest: walnuts in the shell with a nutcracker alongside, or tangerines still attached to their perky green leaves. These all feel like natural gifts of the season.

Sparkling wine or nonalcoholic sparkling cider

Garlic Knot Waffles (page 110)

Rosemary-Almond Salted Caramel Corn (page 29)

A wedge of Gorgonzola Dolce, at room temperature

Chilled fresh red grapes

Green Bean, Watermelon Radish, and Crunchy Quinoa Salad (page 119)

Salt-and-Vinegar Cauliflower and Brussels (page 130)

**Saffron Couscous with Cauliflower, Chickpeas,
and Pomegranate** (page 114)

Roasted Chickens and Schmaltzy-Oven Potatoes (page 159)

Cranberry Meringue Tart (page 207)

Petits Pots de Crème au Café (page 233)

A bowl of walnuts in the shell

Tangerines with leaves

Glühwein (page 266) **with dessert**

When the Party Ends

At some point, after everyone has eaten and drunk as much as they want, the party comes to an end. There are nearly empty wine bottles and loose corks on the table. You've served a salad so delicious that even your most polite guest was eager to take the last serving from the platter. You're sad to see everyone go, but what a sense of accomplishment to have fed your friends, introduced your bestie to your boss, and laughed with everyone when you remembered to pull the tart out of the oven just in the nick of time. Guests say their goodbyes. Maybe a close friend lingers and subtly asks you for that cute guy's number. You know, the one who brought the bouquet of basil from his garden.

A host's chief role is to read the room and anticipate the guests' needs and desires. But unlike the start of the party, which requires a little revving with drinks or introductions or both, when the festivities come to an end, you as the host don't really need to do much. You can offer another round of drinks if it seems like people might want to sip on one more glass. Or try bringing a sweet final bite to the table—something simple that you have in your kitchen like a couple of chocolate bars, broken into randomly shaped pieces, or some fresh fruit. Most people will be happy to eat a few chocolate-covered almonds or to drink a tiny glass of amaro. If you've served a cake or tart for dessert and there's one last slice, try cutting it into many smaller pieces, and you might be surprised how much more likely guests will be to reach for a slice. Nobody ever wants to be the person who takes the last piece, so you just need to make it look like it's not the last piece.

Try not to rush anyone. Let guests thank you for hosting such a fun party. Although, if you do feel like you want to wrap things up (maybe you've got an early morning the next day), you can tell your guests how nice it was to get together, and that'll usually send the subtle message that the party is ending. Clearing plates from the table and washing dishes are other signs that it's time to say goodbye. Don't worry too much about the mess of strewn napkins and empty glasses. Remember that the guests will always mirror the host's energy. So, if you're relaxed, everyone else will be, too.

And what about cleanup? If you're feeling too tired to tackle it right then and there, don't worry, we've all been there. Just get any perishable leftovers into the refrigerator and wrap or cover any foods that can be stored at room temperature. If you have some energy to spare, stack and soak dishes in the kitchen sink. But leave all the glassware out on the countertop or table. You can wash it tomorrow, when there's more light and less likelihood of breakage. One of the sweetest joys of hosting is waking up the next day to find empty glasses abandoned on windowsills, crumpled napkins on chairs, and maybe a stray olive or two that fell to the floor. This detritus means a good time was had by all. It means your guests were comfortable enough to make themselves at home. Take it as a great sign. You did it!

Time to plan the next party.

Sources

INGREDIENTS

Amarena Cherries
MARKET HALL FOODS
markethallfoods.com

Anchovies and Sardines
BELA
belabrandseafood.com

FISHWIFE
eatfishwife.com

JOSÉ
josegourmet.com

ORTIZ
conservasortiz.com

PATAGONIA PROVISIONS
patagoniaprovisions.com

THE SPANISH TABLE
spanishtable.com

WILD PLANET
wildplanetfoods.com

Cheese
BELLWETHER FARMS
bellwetherfarms.com

LAURA CHENEL CHÈVRE
laurachenel.com

MURRAY'S CHEESE
murrayscheese.com

POINT REYES FARMSTEAD
CHEESE CO.
pointreyescheese.com

Chili Crisp
FLY BY JING
flybyjing.com

Chocolate and
Cocoa Powder
GUITTARD CHOCOLATE
COMPANY
guittard.com

KING ARTHUR BAKING
COMPANY
kingarthurbaking.com

VALRHONA
valrhona.com

Dates
RANCHO MELADUCO
DATE FARM
ranchomeladuco.com

Dried Beans, Grains,
and Pasta
ANSON MILLS
ansonmills.com

RANCHO GORDO
ranchogordo.com

SFOGLINI
sfoglini.com

Harissa
NEW YORK SHUK
nyshuk.com

Honey
BEES KNEES
bushwickkitchen.com

BEE RAW
beeraw.com

JACOBSEN CO. HONEY
jacobsensalt.com

KISS THE FLOWER
HONEY CO.
kisstheflower.com

SAVANNAH BEE
COMPANY
savannahbee.com

WEDDERSPOON
wedderspoon.com

ZACH & ZOË SWEET BEE FARM
zachandzoe.co

Masa Harina
MASIENDA
masienda.com

'Nduja, Coppa, and
Other Cured Meats
FRA' MANI
framani.com

LA QUERCIA CURED MEATS
laquerciashop.com

OLYMPIA PROVISIONS
olympiaprovisions.com

Olive Oil
CALIFORNIA OLIVE RANCH
californiaoliveranch.com

ENZO OLIVE OIL COMPANY
enzooliveoil.com

EXAU
exauoliveoil.com

FAT GOLD
fat.gold

PINEAPPLE COLLABORATIVE
pineapplecollaborative.com

SÉKA HILLS
sekahills.com

Orange Blossom Water
NIELSEN-MASSEY
nielsenmassey.com

SAHADI'S
sahadis.com

Pasta
SFOGLINI
sfoglini.com

Salt and Spices
BURLAP & BARREL
burlapandbarrel.com

DIASPORA CO.
diasporaco.com

JACOBSEN SALT CO.
jacobsensalt.com

KALUSTYAN'S
kalustyans.com

MALDON SALT COMPANY
maldonsalt.com

MOONFLOWERS CO
(FOR SAFFRON)
moonflowers.co

OAKTOWN SPICE SHOP
oaktownspiceshop.com

PENZEYS SPICES
penzeys.com

ZINGERMAN'S
zingermans.com

Tahini and Halva
SEED + MILL
seedandmill.com

Tofu
HODO
hodofoods.com

JOODOOBOO
joodooboo.co

DRINKS

Beer
ALE TALES
aletales.beer

ATHLETIC BREWING CO.
(FOR NONALCOHOLIC BEER)
athleticbrewing.com

FIELDWORK
fieldworkbrewing.com

FORT POINT BEER CO.
fortpointbeer.com

ORIGINAL PATTERN
BREWING CO.
originalpatternbeer.com

RUSSIAN RIVER BREWING
COMPANY
russianriverbrewing.com

Spirits
HOME BASE SPIRITS
homebasespirits.com

MADRE MEZCAL
madremezcal.com

ST. AGRESTIS
stagrestis.com

ST. GEORGE SPIRITS
stgeorgespirits.com

UNCLE NEAREST
unclenearest.com

Wine
BROC
broccellars.com

DONKEY & GOAT
donkeyandgoat.com

KERMIT LYNCH WINE
MERCHANT
kermitlynch.com

MARTHA STOUMEN WINES
marthastoumen.com

MINIMO
minimowine.com

ORDINAIRE
ordinairewine.com

RUBY WINE
rubywinesf.com

TOFINO WINES
tofinowines.com

HOME AND KITCHEN SUPPLIES

ANTHROPOLOGIE
anthropologie.com

ÀPLAT
aplat.com

BIG NIGHT
bignightbk.com

BLOCK SHOP
blockshoptextiles.com

BROOK FARM GENERAL STORE
brookfarmgeneralstore.com

CRATE & BARREL
crateandbarrel.com

ESTELLE COLORED GLASS
estellecoloredglass.com

FOOD52
food52.com

GREAT JONES
greatjonesgoods.com

HEATH CERAMICS
heathceramics.com

INDIGO
indigo.ca/en-ca/

MARCH
marchsf.com

MUJI
muji.us

SCHOOLHOUSE
schoolhouse.com

SMEG
smeg.com

SUR LA TABLE
surlatable.com

WILLIAMS SONOMA
williams-sonoma.com

Acknowledgments

I had so much fun making this cookbook. I feel beyond grateful to the many people who worked alongside me to bring the project to life. It's an emotional and humbling experience to put together all these names in one place.

Thank you to my agent and dear friend, Kitty Cowles, for believing in me, pushing me to do my best always, and inspiring me at every turn.

To the team at Artisan: Bella Lemos, Judy Pray, and Lia Ronnen. What an honor and privilege it is to make books with you. Bella, thank you for being the captain of this cookbook ship, for envisioning all the important details, and for making the bookmaking process a total blast. I am thrilled you moved to the East Bay, and I can hardly wait for the parties in our future! Thank you for your insights, wisdom, and extraordinary smarts. Thanks also to Theresa Collier for publicity, Amy Michelson for marketing, Kate Slate for copy editing, Nancy Ringer for proofreading, Nancy Murray and Erica Huang for production, and Hillary Leary for managing editorial.

My appreciation goes to photographer Erin Scott, who captured the exact party vibe I was imagining. Thank you as well to photo assistant Tamer Abu-Dayyeh.

The food in the photographs looks phenomenal thanks to two mega-talented stylists: Nicole Twohy and Amanda Anselmino, with kitchen assists from Genesis Vallejo, Chelsea Lopker, and Huxley McCorkle.

Thank you to Artisan's fabulous design team led by Nina Simoneaux and Suet Chong. Nina executed the layouts, created several new design elements for this book, spearheaded the cover art direction, and put in a huge amount of work to make everything shine. And a very special thank-you to my brilliant husband, Graham Bradley, who drew the custom lettering for the chapter titles and the all-important cover. Wow, am I lucky to be your wife.

Thank you from the bottom of my heart to my family and friends for loving me, supporting me, and cheering me on over the years. One of my not-so-secret-anymore fears of writing this book was that my friends would stop having me over for parties. Because nobody wants the person who wrote the book on parties to come to their party—talk about a buzz kill! But you all are my greatest inspiration. I learned hosting lessons from you, and I continue to marvel at the ways you've made me and so many other guests feel at home. Please promise you'll keep inviting me?

Much love and big thanks to my friends who modeled for the book: Kiersten Turner, Dante Turner, Kristen Miglore, Kristina Cho (who came with a basket of figs from her backyard tree!), Alexia Niparko, Kevin Niparko, Erin Warren, Kevan Warren, Piyush Ghatole, and Elise Carlton (who brought the flowers!). You are gorgeous.

I am also grateful to Bella Lemos, Aya Brackett, the Niparko family, and Mom and Dad for letting me borrow props for the photo shoot.

Thank you to James Bradley for suggesting the greatest party music hits.

The recipes in this book were put through the paces and tested by my most trusted, kitchen-savvy confidantes: Lydia O'Brien and Maddie Kirkby. Thank you both for your tireless efforts and helpful feedback, and thanks for making the work of recipe testing such a joyful endeavor. Every time you told me you loved a dish, my heart did a little cartwheel. Thanks also to Jacob Michael Boynton Welch for lending a hand and a careful eye.

I've been fortunate to collaborate with (and really just be in the general vicinity of) some of the world's best chefs, writers, and thinkers: Suzanne Goin, Alice Waters, Liz Prueitt, Chad Robertson, Roxana Jullapat, Yotam Ottolenghi, Noor Murad, Christina Tosi, Nigel Slater, Nadiya Hussain, Claire Saffitz, Fuchsia Dunlop, Yasmin Khan, Bee Wilson, Pamela Anderson, and Nicola Lamb. Holy smokes, what a lineup. Thank you for your endless inspiration. You are my best friends in the kitchen, and I hear your encouraging voices in my head when I cook.

To Sonia Guerrero, thank you for caring for Arturito (and now baby Lewis!) while I wrote this book. Our family would be lost without you, and we absolutely adore you.

A hug of thanks to all the lovely booksellers who have recommended my previous cookbooks, particularly *The Newlywed Table*. The world is a better place with you in it! Special shout-out to my local independent bookstores, East Bay Booksellers and Mrs. Dalloway's—you make me blush with pride every time I come in to sign a book.

Finally, thank you to my guys: Graham, Arthur, and Lewis. Graham, the person I most want to party with, I know I already thanked you for your work on the design of the book, but I also want to thank you for sticking by my side over the past fifteen years. The seed for this cookbook was planted when I first met you. Thank you for making my life the most beautiful party I could ever have dreamed. I love you and our boys to the moon and back.

Index

Page numbers in *italics* refer to recipe photos.

Photograph by Aya Brackett

Maria Zizka is the author of numerous award-winning cookbooks. She studied biology at UC Berkeley and food culture at UNISG in northern Italy, where she now teaches as a visiting lecturer. She was named by *Forbes* as one of the most influential people under thirty in the world of food and drink. Zizka lives and cooks in the Berkeley Hills with her husband and two sons.